ADULT GUIDANCE SERVICES AND THE LEARNING SOCIETY

Emerging policies in the European Union

Will Bartlett, Teresa Rees and A.G. Watts

The POLICY PRESS

First published in Great Britain in November 2000 by

The Policy Press
University of Bristol
34 Tyndall's Park Road
Bristol BS8 1PY
UK
Tel no +44 (0)117 954 6800
Fax no +44 (0)117 973 7308
E-mail tpp@bristol.ac.uk
www.policypress.org.uk

ISBN 1 86134 153 9

Will Bartlett is Reader in Social Economics at the School for Policy Studies, University of Bristol; **Teresa Rees** is a Professor in the School of Social Sciences, Cardiff University; **A.G. Watts** is Director of the National Institute for Career Education and Counselling.

Cover design by Qube Design Associates, Bristol.

Front cover: photographs supplied by kind permission of www.johnbirdsall.co.uk

Printed in Great Britain by Hobbs the Printers Ltd, Southampton

Contents

Notes on the authors   iv

Preface and acknowledgements   v

List of abbreviations   vii

Part One: The framework

1   Introduction   3

2   What is guidance?   17

3   Learning societies in the European Union   27

Part Two: International comparisons

4   United Kingdom   45

5   English and Scottish case studies   63

6   France   81

7   The Netherlands   97

8   Italy   113

9   Germany   125

Part Three: Key issues

10   Financing adult guidance   145

11   Conclusion   157

References   167

Appendix: Methodological note   179

Notes on the authors

Will Bartlett is Reader in Social Economics at the School for Policy Studies, University of Bristol. His research focuses on welfare reform and quasi-markets. Previous publications include a co-authored book with Julian Le Grand, *Quasi-markets and social policy* (Macmillan, 1993), and two co-edited books: *Quasi-markets and welfare reform* (The Policy Press, 1994) and *A revolution in social policy: Quasi-markets in the 1990s* (The Policy Press, 1997).

Teresa Rees is a Professor in the School of Social Sciences, Cardiff University. She was previously Professor of Labour Market Studies at the School for Policy Studies, University of Bristol. She is a consultant to the European Commission on education, training and labour market policies. Previous publications include *Women and the labour market* (Routledge, 1992); *Mainstreaming equality in the European Union* (Routledge, 1998); *Women and work* (University of Wales Press, 1999) and *Science policies in the European Union: Fostering excellence through mainstreaming gender equality* (with M. Osborn et al) (Office for Official Publications of the European Union, 2000).

Tony Watts is Director of the National Institute for Careers Education and Counselling (NICEC), a network organisation sponsored by the Careers Research and Advisory Centre in Cambridge. Its aims are to develop theory, to inform policy and to enhance practice. He is also Visiting Professor of Career Development at the University of Derby. He has published widely on guidance matters, including recently as co-author of *Rethinking careers education and guidance: Theory, policy and practice* (Routledge, 1996) and *New skills for new futures: Higher education guidance and counselling services in the European Union* (VUB Press, 1998).

Preface and acknowledgements

This book draws on an Economic and Social Research Council (ESRC) funded project *Adult Guidance and the Learning Society* (Grant No RC1105) held by Will Bartlett and Teresa Rees. The project was part of the ESRC's *Learning Society Programme*, directed by Professor Frank Coffield of the University of Newcastle (for an account of findings from the whole programme see Coffield, 2000).

The project examines the impact of the marketisation of adult guidance services in Britain in the context of changing labour markets and policies directed at developing a 'learning society'. Comparisons are made with adult guidance services in France, the Netherlands, Italy and Germany. For all these countries, their location within the European Union (EU) has a bearing on the development of emerging policies: these implications are examined. The book offers an analysis of how variations in adult guidance systems can be linked to the different models of the 'learning society' that inform them. It provides a snapshot at a point in time, illustrating some of the effects of the marketisation of guidance services in the UK on service delivery under the latter years of the Conservative government. Under the Labour government, adult guidance has been linked more with policies geared towards the avoidance of social exclusion. The book concludes with suggestions for how adult guidance could be financed in the UK, drawing on lessons from abroad, and raises some concerns about quality and equity.

Parts of the book have been published elsewhere in article form. Parts of Chapters One and Two are adapted from Watts (1996a) and Watts and Kidd (2000). Case-study material from England features in Bartlett and Rees (1999), from the Netherlands in Rees and Bartlett (1999a), from Scotland in Rees and Bartlett (1999b), and from Germany, France and Britain in Rees et al (1999). The models of the learning society are described in Bartlett and Rees (2000). This book draws together the material from the whole project in a coordinated analytical framework.

The grant holders worked collaboratively with two 'user-partners': Tony Watts, the Director of the National Institute for Careers Education and Counselling, and Cathy Bereznicki, the (then) Chief Executive of the Institute of Careers Guidance (ICG). This book is the result of that collaboration. All three authors are grateful to Cathy for providing expert advice, information, networks and feedback throughout the project. We should also like to acknowledge the valuable advice and support provided by Janice Laird from Fife Adult Guidance and Education Services (FAGES) who coordinates activities on adult guidance for ICG.

We also worked with and are most grateful to our research partners in other EU member states for their guidance and assistance with the fieldwork and its interpretation:

- in the Netherlands – Frans Meijers of the University of Leiden;
- in France – Francis Danvers of the University of Lille, and Nadine Monsanson, a career counsellor-psychologist;
- in Germany – Lynn Chisholm of the European Commission (acting in a private capacity), Marianne Friesse, Barbara Thiessen and Silke Stuckmeyer of the University of Bremen;
- in Italy – Carlo Borzaga of the University of Trento, and Anna Chiesa of the Cooperative Orso in Torino.

In addition, a considerable number of people in these four countries, as well as in the UK, provided significant assistance during the project; we are grateful to them all.

At an ESRC-funded seminar held at the University of Bristol in September 1997, we (with our country consultants) presented our preliminary results to an invited audience of international experts who debated and discussed them, and provided us with valuable feedback. We are grateful to the participants for their contribution to our analysis and interpretation of the results.

Finally, we should like to acknowledge Frank Coffield for his guidance and encouragement, his wit and his wisdom during the life of the project, and The Policy Press for their patience.

List of abbreviations

ACACE	Advisory Council for Adult and Continuing Education
ACIPA	Italian training body
AEGIS	Adult Educational Guidance Initiative in Scotland
AFPA	*Association pour la Formation Professionelle des Adultes* (French Adult Vocational Training Association)
ANPE	*Agence Nationale pour l'Emploi* (French National Employment Agency)
AOB	*Adviesbureas voor Opleiding en Beroep* (Dutch Regional Guidance Bureaux)
APEC	*Association pour l'Emplois des Cadres* (French Association for the Employment of Executives)
BfA	*Bundesanstalt für Arbeit* (German Federal Employment Agency)
bfw	*Berufsfortbildungswerk* (German training organisation)
BIZ	*Berufsberatungs-informationszentrum* (German vocational guidance and information centres)
CBI	Confederation of British Industry
CEC	Commission of the European Communities
CfBT	Centre for British Teachers
CIBC	*Centre Interinstitutionel de Bilans de Compétences* (French Inter-Institutional Skills Assessment Centre)
CIG	*Cassa Integrazione Guadagni* (Italian Wage Supplementation Fund)
CIGO	Italian Wage Supplementation Fund – ordinary
CIGS	Italian Wage Supplementation Fund – special
CILO	*Centri di Iniziativa Locale per l'Occupazione*
CIO	*Centres d'Information et Orientation* (French Careers Information Offices)
CNA	*Confederazione Nazionale dell'Artigianato* (National Confederation of Artisans)
CORA	*Centri Orientamento Retravailler*
DENI	Department of Education for Northern Ireland
DES	Department of Education and Science
DF	*Donne e Formazione* (Italian training organisation for women returners)
DfEE	Department for Education and Employment
DG	Directorate General of European Commission

EC	European Commission
ECCTIS	Educational Counselling and Credit Transfer Information Service
EDAP	Employee Development Assistance Programme
EGSA	Educational Guidance Services for Adults
ES	Employment Service
ESF	European Social Fund
ESOL	English for Speakers of Other Languages
ESRC	Economic and Social Research Council
EU	European Union
EURES	Network of Employment Services (from the member states)
FAGES	Fife Adult Guidance and Education Service
FE	further education
FEDORA	*Forum Européen de l'Orientation Académique*
FEFC	Further Education Funding Council
FEPS	free entry, pay to stay
FONGECIF	*Fond Gestion Congé Individuel Formation* (French employers' training fund)
GAB	Guidance Accreditation Board
GDP	Gross Domestic Product
GIP	*Groupement d'Interest Publique* (French public interest organisation)
HE	higher education
HMI	Her Majesty's Inspectorate
IAGA	Information, Advice and Guidance for Adults
ICG	Institute of Careers Guidance
ILAs	Individual Learning Accounts
INETOP	*L'Institut National d'Etude du Travail et d'Orientation Professionelle* (National Institute for the Study of Work and Professional Guidance)
LASA	*Land* of Brandenburg Agency for Structure and Labour Ltd
LDC	*Landelijk Dienstverlendend Centrum* (Dutch National Careers Guidance Information Centre)
LEA	local education authority
LECs	Local Enterprise Companies
MLs	*Missions Locales*
MoD	Ministry of Defence
NACCEG	National Advisory Council for Careers and Educational Guidance (the Guidance Council)

NACRO	National Association for the Care and Rehabilitation of Offenders
NAEGA	National Association for Educational Guidance for Adults
NCGE	National Centre for Guidance in Education
NHS	National Health Service
NICEC	National Institute for Careers Education and Counselling
NIP	Netherlands Institute of Psychologists
NOW	New Opportunities for Women
NVQ	National Vocational Qualification
NVS	*Nederlandse Verniging van Schooldekanen* (Dutch Federation of Careers Teachers)
OCW	*Ministerie van Onderwijs, Cultuur en Wetenschappen* (Dutch Ministry Department of Education)
OECD	Organisation for Economic Co-operation and Development
ONISEP	French National Office for Information on Education and Occupations
PAIO	*Permanence d'Acceuil d'Information et d'Orientation* (French Offices for Advice, Information and Guidance)
RTCs	*Regionale Opleidingen Centra* (Dutch Regional Training Centres)
SAL	*Servizio Accompagnamento al Lavoro* (Italian initiative run by SAL)
SCAGES	Standing Conference of Associations for Guidance in Educational Settings
SME	small and medium-sized enterprise
SPEC	Support Programme for Employment Creation
SRB	Single Regeneration Budget
SQMS	Scottish Quality Management System for Education and Training
SZW	*Ministerie van Sociale Zaken en Wekgelenheid* (Dutch Ministry of Employment)
T&EA	Training and Employment Agency
TECs	Training and Enterprise Councils
TUC	Trades Union Congress
UDACE	Unit for the Development of Adult Continuing Education
UfI	University for Industry
UPLMO	Italian local employment offices

YMCA	Young Men's Christian Association
ZIP	*Koordinierungs- und Beratungsstelle Frau und Beruf – Zurück in den Beruf* (German Coordination and Advice Bureau: Women and Work – Back to Work)

Part One:
The framework

ONE

Introduction

This book is concerned with emerging policies towards the delivery of adult guidance services within the UK, and in contrasted European Union (EU) member states. Guidance services should be assuming a more significant role than in the past, given some of the trends in the European labour market and policies designed to foster 'lifelong learning'. Sustained concern about levels of unemployment in the EU, combined with fiscal imperatives to reduce public spending on welfare, should also trigger renewed interest in the efficiency of guidance services that seek to relate people to appropriate education, training and employment opportunities. Adult guidance services lie at the intersection of economic, social, education, training and welfare policy development.

A wide variety of approaches to the provision of career guidance services is in evidence in the various member states of the EU (Watts et al, 1993). The research project on which this book is based took as its starting point the major changes to public-sector services introduced in the UK in the mid-1990s, during the latter years of the Conservative government. These changes included the introduction of 'quasi-market' principles for the delivery of statutory services. Under a quasi-market, services continue to be publicly funded but can be delivered by new providers, including those from the private sector, who successfully bid for contracts. While adult guidance services in the UK are not part of statutory provision, they were profoundly influenced by quasi-market changes to one of the major providers – careers services.

To position these policy developments in the UK, the research project included studies of adult guidance services in four other EU member states, chosen to illustrate diversity and divergence among systems and approaches. We examined:

- the pluralistic model found in France;
- the centralised state-managed system found in Germany;
- the more decentralised system, based largely on non-profit providers, found in Italy;
- the more market-based approach adopted in the Netherlands.

All these systems are operating within the context of the Single Market and EU policies designed to contribute to the enhancement of economic competitiveness, the avoidance of social exclusion and the fostering of a 'learning society'. Crucial issues emerge in the comparison of adult guidance services and of policies to develop these services, including concerns about funding, access, quality and equity.

Framework for the book

The book is divided into three sections, the first of which sets out our framework for analysis. This first chapter describes the labour-market and welfare-reform contexts within which guidance services are operating. We consider the effects of labour-market and welfare-reform changes on the concept of a 'career', and outline our three models of a learning society, which we identify as informing policies for adult guidance in the individual member states and indeed in the EU itself. Special emphasis is laid on quasi-markets in welfare reform, given its significance in the UK and to some extent in two of our case-study countries, France and the Netherlands. This brings us to the focus of Chapter Two, which explores the complex question, 'what is guidance?'. Then, in Chapter Three, we look at how EU policies to promote a learning society bear upon adult guidance services in the member states.

Part Two focuses on international comparisons. It begins with an overview of adult guidance in the UK from the mid-1990s to the present day (Chapter Four). We next report on the findings of our research on the organisation of guidance services in our UK case-study areas, four of which are in England and one in Scotland (Chapter Five). Subsequent chapters in this section examine France (Chapter Six), the Netherlands (Chapter Seven), Italy (Chapter Eight) and Germany (Chapter Nine). The English and Scottish case studies are based on interviews with key actors, field visits to a range of providers in the area and an analysis of documents and statistics (for further information on the methodology used in the study, see the Appendix). In the four other EU countries, we took a similar approach but worked closely with national experts (listed in the acknowledgements) to construct the country descriptions and collect data from key actors and providers.

The accounts, of course, represent a snapshot in time in a field where policy is inevitably changing rapidly. Fieldwork was conducted in France, Italy and Germany in 1996 and in the Netherlands and the UK in 1997. The significance of the results lies more in the opportunity provided for constructing a broad comparative analysis for the development of models, rather than as a source of up-to-the-minute descriptions of current practice. Nevertheless, the major developments in the UK since the change of government in 1997 are identified in Chapter Four, in particular the increasing divergence in approaches in England, Scotland, Wales and Northern Ireland since devolution.

Part Three of the book returns to the analytical framework to address some of the issues raised. One of the key issues is who should pay for adult guidance services, when arguably the individual, colleges, employers and indeed the state could all be seen as beneficiaries of an effective service (Chapter Ten). A series of alternatives are proposed for the UK, drawing on our international fieldwork. However, this debate, in turn, entails returning to the question 'what is guidance?', and whether a differentiation should be made between information provision and more in-depth individual or group counselling services. In the final chapter (Chapter Eleven), we return to some of the concerns about the impact of welfare reforms (principally quasi-markets) on quality and equity. We also assess the extent to which changes in the systems of provision of guidance services are consistent with one or more of the models of the learning society outlined later in this introductory chapter.

The remaining sections of this chapter, then, address contextual factors. We discuss, firstly, the labour-market context within which adult guidance services are operating. Secondly, we look at the changing concept of career. Thirdly, we present our three models of the learning society. Finally, we examine the context of welfare reforms that have affected the funding and delivery of public services, focusing especially on the introduction of quasi-markets to parts of the public sector.

The labour-market context

A central feature of contemporary capitalism is the increasing awareness of uncertainty, risk and insecurity. Despite an almost unprecedented world-wide boom that until recently seemed to defy conventional concepts of the business cycle, mass consumer demand is constrained by a widespread fear of unemployment. Labour markets, adapting to the twin pressures of globalisation and technological change, have become more turbulent and flexible, and labour contracts have become increasingly fixed-term or part-time (Hutton, 1995). In many areas of industry, old concepts of a 'job for life' have begun to break down. Labour-market participants increasingly expect to make frequent job changes and indeed occupational changes in the course of their working lives (CSJ/IPPR, 1994). In the new service industries – the most dynamic sector of modern economies – the need for flexibility and adaptability to accommodate ever-changing consumer fashions creates an in-built impermanence of employment. The greatest share of new job creation in most advanced economies is accounted for in the growing sector of small and medium-sized businesses, but these jobs often disappear almost as rapidly as they are created, since the bulk of small businesses collapse before they reach maturity (Storey, 1994). At the same time, rapid technological change is creating a demand for an ever more highly skilled labour force. Individuals are faced with the need to develop new skills, to retrain and to periodically re-engage with the institutions of formal education. Modern capitalism has been referred to as a 'risk society' (Beck, 1992).

In the UK, Conservative government policy in the 1980s and 1990s actively promoted deregulation of the labour market, reducing the employment protection previously granted to the workforce. Companies 'downsized' and 'delayered', reducing the size of their core permanent staff and increasing their employment of part-time and contract workers. In 1993, just over half the labour force could expect to remain in the same job for less than five years.

These changes have not, of course, affected all sections of the labour market with equal force. Overall, there has been little change in the average duration of job tenure (Burgess and Rees, 1996, 1997; Doogan, 1998). However, this observation disguises substantial shifts in career patterns among different segments of the labour force. Job security for male workers, measured by median length of job tenure, fell by 20% between 1975 and 1993, and labour turnover has risen dramatically both for older workers and for less skilled men (Gregg and Wadsworth, 1995). The decrease in length of job tenure for men has been offset by an increase in the length of job tenure for women, but this is in a context in which women, in any case, have a much higher share of part-time and temporary work. While a hard core of permanent employees has been insulated from these effects, there is much greater instability among secondary-labour-market participants in part-time work, self-employment and other forms of 'atypical' work. Even within the core labour force, there is evidence of change. Comparing the recessions of 1980-82 and 1989-92, Inkson (1995) found that the proportion of managers changing jobs each year had increased from 21% to 30%, while 'discontinuities' in managers' career paths, due to job severance, were an increasingly common experience among managerial personnel.

In the EU in the mid–1990s, rates of job turnover averaged just over 16%, indicating that on average one in six workers changed their job each year (EC, 1998). The rate of job turnover tended to be lower among younger age groups (15–24 years old) than among older workers, but was similar for men and women. Turnover rates did, however, vary markedly across countries; they were relatively high in the UK and relatively low in Italy. For example, only 7% of men aged 25 to 49 changed their jobs in Italy in 1996, compared to 15% of men in that age group in the UK. Looked at another way, 45% of men in this age group in Italy had held their current job for more than 10 years, compared to only 32% in the UK. France, Germany and the Netherlands lay between these two extremes.

Furthermore, changes from one job to another increasingly involve transitions between different types of jobs with different skill requirements, and between employment and retraining, rather than simple lay-off and re-hire into the same place of employment, or even into the same industry or occupation. For example, in 1996, in the EU as a whole, the proportion of workers who changed their jobs within a year and took up a job in another sector (4%) was just the same as the proportion who changed jobs and remained within the same sector (EC, 1998). As a result, the transition between jobs in the flexible labour market is closely connected to periodic entry and re entry into spells of education and training.

A further dimension of labour-market flexibility is the increase in non–standard employment, such as teleworking and the growth in part-time work. Employees negotiate their own flexible arrangements (see Collin and Watts, 1996). The growth in 24-hour cover, especially in the expanding service sector, and new EU directives on hours of work, parental leave and part-time hours, are likely to have further implications for individuals' patterns of working. This in turn implies a different relationship between employers and their employees and prompts a revisit to the concept of career, focused around Watts' (1996a) analysis of what he terms the 'careerquake'.

The concept of career and the 'psychological contract'

The effect of the various trends in the labour market (risk and uncertainty, flexible and non-standard working) is a profound change in the 'psychological contract' between the individual and the organisation –

their perceptions of the obligations each has to the other (Argyris, 1960). The traditional contract was a long-term *relational* one, based on security and reciprocal loyalty; this has largely broken down. Now the contract tends increasingly to be a short-term *transactional* one, based on a narrower and more purely economic exchange. Where the relational contract survives, it commonly involves exchanging job security for greater task flexibility (Herriot and Pemberton, 1995).

In either case, therefore, the contract now requires regular renegotiation. It also pressurises individuals to take more responsibility for their own career development, including learning new skills and knowledge. Security, it is argued, lies now not in *employment* but in *employability*; accumulating skills and reputation that can be invested in new opportunities as they arise (Kanter, 1989). This leads to the notion that individuals, whether formally self-employed or not, should *regard* themselves as self-employed, taking responsibility for their own career-long self-development (Bridges, 1995; Hakim, 1994).

A key policy issue is whether it is possible to reconcile such flexibility with social cohesion. For some, flexibility is a euphemism for naked exercise of labour-market power: workers' labour can be exploited on low wages, with no benefits and no security, and they can then be thrown back on to the labour market – without any sense of corporate responsibility – when their labour is no longer needed. The combination of flexible labour markets, high employment and poverty traps induced by current social-security arrangements means that unemployment is increasingly concentrated in particular households and communities. There is a growing divide between work-rich families, with several incomes, and no-work families surviving on a mixture of welfare benefits, undeclared cash-in-hand payments for odd jobs, and petty crime. Many of these families are concentrated on estates with low-quality housing, and high levels of social disorder and criminal activity. Such divisions threaten a decline into an ever more splintered, violent society, which reduces the quality of life for all (see Wilkinson, 1996).

The vital question, therefore, is whether it is possible to devise ways of yielding the potential benefits of labour-market flexibility, and making these benefits more widely available, while minimising its risks and dangers. Arguably, the key to reconciling social equity and upgrading of skills with a flexible labour market is a much broader concept of career, supported by appropriate social institutions and incentives. Instead of being viewed narrowly as progression up the hierarchy within an organisation or profession, a career can be viewed as the individual's lifelong progression in learning and in work. The breadth of these terms is important. 'Learning' embraces not only formal education and training, but also informal methods of learning, in the workplace and elsewhere. 'Work' includes not only paid employment and self-employment, but also many other forms of socially valuable work, in households and in the community (including child-rearing and caring for older people). 'Progression' covers not only vertical but also lateral movement; it is concerned with experience as well as positions, and with broadening as well as advancing. 'Progression' does, however, retain the sense of development; career is more than mere biography.

This represents what Collin and Watts (1996) have called the "death and transfiguration of career". Unlike the old bureaucratic concept, which was by definition élitist in nature, the new definition could in principle be accessible to all. It could provide a framework for encouraging all individuals to continue to learn and develop throughout life, linked to a sense of having a stake in the society of which they are part. It would thus make it possible for the whole population to participate in – and benefit from – the upgrading of skills which countries need in order to achieve international competitiveness (Porter, 1990). In this sense, it could make it possible to reconcile flexibility with a just society, in Rawls' (1972) challenging definition of the term: a society we would choose to live in even if we did not know what position within it we ourselves would occupy.

If a career in this broader sense is to be available to all, policy interventions are required (Watts, 1996a). One of these is a more flexible social welfare system. But many of the others are related to learning. Learning is the key to progression in work. If individuals are to be able to move from work contract to work contract with a sense of development rather than mere survival, they need to find ways of enhancing their skills and knowledge on a continuing basis. Some companies are now developing a new 'psychological contract', in which they seek to offer employees security not by offering a 'job for life' but by providing training and development opportunities that will extend their marketable skills and sustain their 'career resilience' (Waterman et al, 1994; Kessler and Undy, 1996). This needs to be part of a more flexible and responsive learning system, supported by an integrated qualification framework, providing a clear and widely recognised climbing-frame for career development.

A key component of such a policy framework is lifelong access to career guidance. If individuals are to secure progression in their learning and work within the fragmented world of flexible labour markets, career guidance is crucial. A massive increase is needed both in the quantity of such guidance and in its quality.

Within the industrial era, the role of career guidance has been limited. It has largely been selection processes that have determined the destiny of individuals, both within the education system and within the employment system. Career guidance has been a limited switch mechanism to fine-tune the passage from one system to the other. That is why career guidance services have been largely concentrated around the transition from full-time education to employment. In practice, the two systems have usually been so well synchronised that it has not had too much to do. It has been, in general, a marginal and low-status activity.

Now, however, its role is moving centre-stage. If individuals are to take responsibility for their career development, career guidance is critical. This is the case in three respects: in helping individuals to clarify and articulate their aims and aspirations; in ensuring that their decisions are informed in relation to the needs of the labour market; and in empowering individuals in their negotiations with employers and other purchasers of their services. Concentrating such guidance resources at the entry-point to employment is no longer adequate. Careers are now based, not on a single decision point, but on a long series of iterative decisions made throughout people's lives. Guidance needs to be available at all these decision points.

Models of the learning society

The centrality of learning is increasingly being framed in the concept of the 'learning society'. There are, however, different models of what this concept represents (Rees and Bartlett, 1999a).

One influential view argues that the key to success in the modern hyper-competitive global economy is the development of the skills of the labour force (Reich, 1992; Commission on Public Policy and British Business, 1997). The competitive advantage of nations is no longer to be found solely in the accumulation of either physical or financial capital that is globally mobile, but in the acquisition of skills and knowledge that have become the new scarce resource. Even these are not enough. With rapid technological change, it is the ability to re-skill and re-train the labour force which is held to distinguish the more successful economies from the less successful. We call this approach the *skills growth model* of the learning society.

There are, however, a variety of other views of what a learning society should be, or should aim to achieve. Some commentators are sceptical of an overly simplistic and deterministic link between improvements in skills and the achievement of more rapid economic growth. Instead, they point to the need for a more voluntaristic approach, in which the aim of the learning society should be an increase in capacities to achieve individual self-fulfilment in all spheres of life, not just in economic activities. This approach highlights a concern for equity (Keep and Mayhew, 1996), designed to supplement the search for greater efficiency emphasised by those who focus on the link between skill formation and economic growth. We refer to this second approach as the *personal development model* of the learning society.

There is also a third view, which to some extent addresses both concerns, and which emphasises the role of institutions of trust and cooperation in promoting economic growth on an equitable basis. In this view, it is not human capital (training, education) but rather social capital (networks, communications and the strength of civil society) that is the binding constraint to the effective deployment of accumulated capital, skills and other resources in pursuit of economic growth (Putnam, 1993a, 1993b; Fukuyama, 1995). However, such social capital can only be developed through a process of social learning (Wilson, 1997), a process which offers a more participative and community-based approach to the development of a learning society. We call this third approach the *social learning model* of the learning society.

The concept of a learning society is a highly contested one (Coffield, 1998). Nevertheless, whatever one's view concerning the form that a learning society should take, its effectiveness is likely to depend significantly on the ability of individuals to make informed choices about employment, education and training opportunities on a continual basis. If lifelong learning is to become a reality, accessible ports of entry and routes of progression will be needed in education and training systems. Individuals will increasingly be expected to create their own trajectories between education, training, employment, unemployment and non-employment, combining learning activities with different employment statuses. Career guidance services have been traditionally oriented towards helping school leavers manage their initial transition from education to working life. However, such services will increasingly be required to provide information, advice, counselling and other forms of support to adults, as they traverse a flexible career path between a variety of jobs and between a variety of economic and social roles. Services will also need to have the capacity to assist individuals to make choices between the burgeoning variety of education and training opportunities and opportunity providers. There appears to be a growing consensus on the importance of career guidance for adults as an active and central element in its development. This is a view expressed, for example, by the National Advisory Group for Continuing Education and Lifelong Learning, which argues that "the provision of up-to-date, accessible and impartial information and advice will be essential if a strategy of lifelong learning for all is to be successful" (Fryer, 1997, p 8). However, there are different ideas as to how it should be delivered.

The conceptual model of the form that a learning society should take has significant implications for the appropriate mode of delivery, structure and operation of guidance services. In the skills growth model, guidance services can be seen primarily as providing a 'brokerage' service, between adults seeking a suitable niche in the labour market or in the education and training markets, and employers seeking employees or learning providers recruiting students or trainees. Such services can be described as seeking to facilitate the smooth operation of the labour market and the associated emerging 'learning market'. In the personal development model, the role of job matching is played down. Rather, guidance is needed at all points on a career path, not just at points of transition. This underpins the idea of guidance being for employed people, as well as for new entrants, the unemployed and returnees. This approach is consistent with schemes such as the Ford Employee Development Assistance Programme (EDAP) scheme, which gives employees opportunities for personal development training as well as narrow occupational training. In the third model, social learning, the role of the guidance worker is one of facilitator of social action rather than one of simple job matching or of guiding personal development on an individualised basis. Guidance is integrated with social action and is consistent with the growth of third-sector providers (eg social cooperatives, voluntary organisations) which interact with users, not only to improve access to the job and learning markets, but also to facilitate a social learning process and promote community development. Of course, these various approaches are not necessarily mutually exclusive and may operate alongside each other in a complementary way. In most countries there is mix of various modes of provision, but the mix varies from one country to another. The underlying model of a learning society behind the policies of the EU appears to be the 'skills growth model'. We will return to these three models in our concluding chapter when comparing our international case studies.

Welfare reform and the development of quasi-markets

Guidance services are not only affected by government policies (at both EU and UK levels) designed to enhance economic activity rates and combat unemployment and social exclusion, but also operate in a context of welfare reform. There was a considerable programme of such reform in most EU member states during the 1990s, in an attempt to reduce public expenditure. The high and persistent levels of unemployment described above led to a series of measures designed to reduce the benefit bill. The pressure on national economies induced by the conditions laid down to join the European Monetary Union also fuelled attempts to reduce public spending. Active labour-market policies, including adult guidance provision, have been regarded as more cost-effective than simply supporting the unemployed through benefit provision (Ducatel et al, 2000). In the UK, the Conservative government re categorised those in receipt of unemployment benefit as 'job seekers', who then were obliged to demonstrate their availability for work and to provide evidence of their job-seeking activities. The Labour government continued this policy but added New Deal, an initiative targeted at the young unemployed and single mothers in the first instance, but now extended to other target groups including the adult long-term unemployed, as part of its US-inspired welfare-to-work campaign (see Chapter Four).

A significant element of the approach to welfare reform in the UK was the marketisation of some elements of the public services by the Conservative government. 'Quasi-markets' were established in many areas of public service such as health, education and social care (Le Grand and Bartlett, 1993). In these quasi-markets, services continued to be funded through public finance and were delivered free at the point of delivery. Provision was decentralised, however, and independent provider organisations were established, both on a 'for-profit' and on a 'not-for-profit' basis. An essential element of the quasi-market arrangement was the creation of competition between providers, designed to mimic the operation of a competitive market. The defining characteristic of quasi-market mechanisms was not privatisation per se but rather marketisation, the attempt to mimic market mechanisms within a publicly funded system. In addition, service providers were constrained in their freedoms through a system of stringent regulation (Walsh, 1995).

Two basic methods of quasi-market competition were introduced. In the first method, service providers competed for contracts to run their service. Competition took place for the right to deliver services to the clients (examples included contracts between NHS trusts and their purchasers – local health authorities or general practitioner fundholders – as well as the contracted-out career guidance services discussed in Chapters Four and Five). In the second method, providers competed among themselves directly for clients, who would be issued with vouchers, or whose patronage would trigger a capitation payment (examples included the formula funding of schools in proportion to the number of enrolled pupils and the capitation payments to general practitioners, as well as some experiments – mentioned in Chapter Four – with the use of vouchers in the delivery of guidance services).

An essential element of the quasi-market approach to the provision of public-sector services was the use of competition as an instrument to improve efficiency and responsiveness, and to provide choice to users of the services. Such competition does not necessarily have to be actualised; potential competition can sometimes produce the same effects. Baumol et al (1982) have emphasised that contestability of markets is the essential element; that is to say, the threat of new entry is enough to ensure that existing providers will maintain competitive levels of cost and quality. If entry is feasible, new entrants can capture existing market position of incumbents who earn excess profits by cost-cutting and reducing quality. In the absence of free entry, as in the case of many publicly contracted services, ex ante competition may be replaced by ex post monopoly, once the contract is awarded. Hence the need for periodic re-contracting and for contract-compliance mechanisms during the life of the contract.

Contracts are often very loosely specified, in the form of a block contract that provides a global budget and a requirement to deliver a certain number of services of different types. Sometimes more tightly specified contracts are designed which offer a fixed price for a unit of service. Block contracts potentially shift risk onto the provider, who has to bear the cost of any cost over-run. Cost-per-case contracts shift risk to the purchaser, who has to meet the cost of an uncertain demand for services. One solution to the risk-sharing dilemma lies in designing mixed contracts that share risks between the purchaser and the provider. Such contracts have a core block element, but also some element of cost-per-case contracting.

Another solution to the problem of risk and uncertainty can be found in the creation of long-term relationships between purchaser and provider. Such relationships provide a framework within which risk and uncertainty can be managed. Providers can be assured that their long-term strategic goals can be accommodated within a framework of cooperation and trust, and that they are not going to be penalised for short-term failures by losing their contract and being forced out of business. In this environment, they are able to make long-term plans and are encouraged to make investments for the future.

In the UK, local-authority careers services were privatised under the Conservative government. Quasi-markets were introduced through the creation of independent provider units that competed for contracts to run a service in a defined geographical area. Ownership of the careers services was transferred to new, private careers companies. In many cases, these were based on the old local education authority (LEA) careers services, transformed into new, private, limited-liability shareholder companies. Such companies were, in most cases, not-for-profit organisations, and the shareholders were commonly public entities, such as LEAs and Training and Enterprise Councils (TECs) in England and Wales, or Local Enterprise Companies (LECs) in Scotland. The contracts involved a mixed system of payments. A core block contract funded the provision of guidance services for school leavers and other young people, while a targeted cost-per-case element was also included for a proportion of the contract, linked to the number of action plans delivered to clients. In addition, careers companies were free to increase their income by providing commercial services to various client groups within specified market segments, including adults.

The critique of risk and uncertainty in the case of short-term periodic contracting is relevant to the design of this contract system. It involved short-term contracts with periodic recontracting, which gave little incentive to providers to engage in long-term investment in improvement of the services. It was replaced by the incoming Labour government in 1997 with a system of licensing, with re-contracting only in the case of a failure to meet the regulatory conditions of the contract. These regulations included the imposition of targets, which tended to distort the allocation of providers' efforts in the direction of the targets.

In summary, the privatised careers companies in the UK have operated in both a quasi-market and a real market. A quasi-market was established by requiring the careers companies to compete for contracts for the right to deliver a service to the core statutory group of school pupils and school leavers. A real market has also begun to emerge for adults, since the careers companies have had the right to charge fees to their adult users for their services. The impact of the privatisation of the careers service and its effects on adult guidance in the UK are discussed in greater detail in Chapter Four. Although the emphasis in the UK in recent years has been on the creation of quasi-market forms of public-service delivery, it should be emphasised that such quasi-markets are by no means the only way to organise the efficient and equitable delivery and financing of public services. As we show in subsequent chapters, the European experience provides a rich mix of diverse approaches to the organisation of guidance services.

Conclusion

In this book, we consider the changing forms of guidance in different European countries. Labour-market trends, the end of the psychological contract and welfare reforms have focused a new attention on guidance services and their role in developing learning societies. Individuals face increasing uncertainties when they try to negotiate their labour-market trajectories. Sectoral shifts, increasingly diverse and flexible patterns of employment and the emphasis on skilling and re-skilling put pressure on individuals sequentially to reposition themselves. Guidance services that have traditionally focused on the initial transition from education to working life face the challenge of addressing this new context.

The pattern of service provision and their sources of funding varies considerably among member states. In some countries, state provision is important. In others, market or quasi-market forms of provision can be found in which services remain publicly-funded and are provided to users without charge, but are delivered on a competitive basis by a range of independent public, private or third-sector providers. The purpose of a quasi-market of this type is to induce synthetic market competition between providers of public services in the hope that this will improve the efficiency with which services are delivered to the public (Le Grand and Bartlett, 1993). Elsewhere, there has been a trend towards the full marketisation of adult guidance services, making a market of the market brokers (Watts, 1995). In such cases, efforts have been made to develop a genuine market in which users pay for services, but there may be an element of public subsidy involved in order to stimulate demand. In the case of the UK, combinations of both these methods have been implemented at different stages of the guidance process, with free information being combined with user fees for more in-depth guidance services. Differences in country-specific methods of organising guidance services are likely to reflect to some extent the underlying model of the learning society that policy makers are trying to implement. However, before we can examine these country differences in more detail, it is important to address the question of what is meant by guidance.

TWO

What is guidance?

Introduction

To provide a basis for the subsequent chapters, it is necessary to examine more carefully what is meant by guidance, and some of the competing ways in which the concept is constructed. A broad definition is that it comprises a range of processes designed to enable individuals to make informed choices and transitions relating to learning and work. Most lay people tend to identify guidance with information, assessment and advice-giving within individual interviews. Interview sessions are, however, only one of the settings for guidance; others include self-help and group sessions. The activities that can take place within these settings are also more varied than popular stereotypes suggest.

An influential list of seven activities was developed by the Unit for the Development of Adult Continuing Education (UDACE, 1986), which comprised informing, advising, counselling, assessing, enabling, advocating and feeding back. This drew from an earlier list (Watts, 1980) but focused more narrowly on educational guidance services for adults; accordingly, it omitted careers education, so tending to detach guidance from the curriculum. Subsequently, the Standing Conference of Associations for Guidance in Educational Settings (SCAGES, 1993) produced an expanded list. This was designed to cover guidance in all educational settings, and therefore reintroduced careers education (as 'teaching') and also added more managerial activities designed to coordinate guidance activities and integrate them into organisational contexts. The full SCAGES list of eleven activities is shown in Figure 1. Although developed for use in educational settings, it is in principle transferable to other settings too, including work and community settings.

Within this definition, a number of potential 'fault lines' can be identified which have been the source of professional contestation within the guidance field and of lay confusion outside it. Five are particularly noteworthy: between educational and vocational guidance; between directive and non-directive approaches; between separate and integrated approaches; between reactive and proactive approaches; and between guidance and placement (Watts and Kidd, 2000).

Figure 1: Guidance activities

Informing
Providing information about opportunities available, without any discussion of the relative merits of options for particular individuals.

Advising
Helping learners to interpret information and choose the most appropriate option. To benefit from advice, individuals must already have a fairly clear idea of what their needs are.

Counselling
Working with learners as individuals to help them to discover, clarify, assess and understand their own experience, and to explore alternatives and their possible implementation. Counselling is a purposeful activity deliberately entered into by both the learner and counsellor, and is learner-led. It may involve a series of regular contacts.

Assessing
Helping learners, by formal or informal means, to obtain a structured understanding of their personal, educational and vocational development in order to enable them to make informed judgements about the appropriateness of particular opportunities.

Teaching
Providing a planned and systematic progression of learner-centred experiences to enable learners to acquire knowledge, skills and competencies related to making personal, educational and career decisions and transitions.

Enabling
Supporting learners in dealing with agencies providing or influencing learning/employment opportunities. This may, for example, involve helping learners with making applications, or negotiating changes in arrangements.

Advocating
Negotiating directly with institutions or agencies on behalf of specific learners for whom there may be additional barriers to access (eg negotiating exceptional entry arrangements).

Networking
Establishing specific links with a range of individuals and agencies to support and enhance guidance work with learners. These links may be formal or informal, but will include regular contact for information exchange, referral and feedback, and other joint activities such as staff development, monitoring and review, and outreach work.

Feeding back
Gathering and collating information on the unmet needs of learners, and encouraging providers of opportunities to respond by adapting or developing their provision. This may involve practical changes (eg in presentation of information) or organisational ones (eg redesigning opportunities to meet the needs of particular learner groups).

Managing
Managing guidance activities into a coherent programme, ensuring it is sustainable within its institutional or organisational setting, coordinating and developing its human and physical resources, evaluating its effectiveness, and promoting its service and interests.

Innovating/systems change
Supporting the development of the curriculum, changes in institutional practice and changes in guidance practice, in order to maintain and improve the quality of both educational and guidance provision.

Source: SCAGES (1993)

The first distinction, *between educational and vocational guidance*, cuts across the full set of activities by distinguishing between choices relating to learning and to work respectively. Both form part of the generic activity which we refer to as 'career guidance' ('career' rather than 'careers' in order to emphasise the variable nature of career paths through a lifetime of shifting employment and training experiences). Often but not always provided by the same organisations and professionals, educational guidance provides services particularly on entry into education and training, while vocational guidance provides services particularly on exit from these, as well as to unemployed people seeking work, and to employed people seeking a career change. In principle, such choices are closely interwoven, and much guidance is concerned with their inter-relationship. This is particularly the case if broad definitions are adopted both of learning and of work, as suggested in Chapter One:

- learning as covering not only education and training, but also informal learning in a wide variety of settings;
- work as covering not only employment and self-employment, but also unpaid work in the household and community.

Career guidance is an umbrella term that can usefully cover progression in learning and work in all these various forms. In practice, however, there has been a tendency for educational guidance to become institutionalised in a separate form – particularly within colleges and universities, and in educational guidance services for adults. In part this can be seen as a defence of professional territory; in part as a means of resisting the incursions of vocationalism into educational concerns. It tends to be defended by invoking the legitimacy of non-vocational motivations for learning, including intrinsic rather than extrinsic motivations. A broad definition of career guidance can, and should, embrace such motivations. But the term tends to be defined in a more narrow way by those intent on restricting its territorial boundaries in order to remain outside them.

The second distinction is *between directive and non-directive approaches*. Prior to the 1960s, guidance tended to be directive in nature, and focused heavily on assessment and advice-giving. It was based on the methods of differential psychology, matching individuals to occupations (Rodger, 1952); the task of guidance was seen as being to *diagnose* the individual's attributes and to *prescribe* appropriate opportunities. The influence of Rogerian counselling (Rogers, 1965), linked with the application to career guidance of the insights of developmental psychology (Super, 1957), led to a markedly different approach in which the task was seen as being to *facilitate* the individual's decision-making processes and to *develop* their own decision-making skills. Accordingly, it laid more emphasis on counselling and on careers education. Some adherents of counselling approaches, indeed, tend to distance themselves from the whole concept of 'guidance', regarding it as being directive in nature and therefore inimical to counselling approaches. The SCAGES (1993) definition, however, implicitly contests this; it adopts as one of its primary principles that "the aim of guidance is to enable learners to take full responsibility for their own decisions and the implementation of actions arising from those decisions" (p 36). It views counselling as one, but only one, of the range of activities through which this aim can be pursued. Its definition of 'assessing', for example, lays emphasis not on diagnosis and prescription but on informing the individual's own self-understanding.

The third distinction is *between separate and integrated approaches*. The UDACE (1986) definition was limited not only in its focus on educational opportunities but also in viewing guidance as being outside mainstream educational provision, supporting individuals in their transactions with such provision. The SCAGES (1993) definition incorporated this view, but recognised that guidance could also be an integral part of educational provision, in two respects. The first is as part of the curriculum, either in an 'enclosed' sense (eg a separate course in careers education) or in a more 'systemic' sense, permeating the curriculum and making it subject to negotiation with the individual learner (Watts and Young, 1997). The second is as part of the organisational structure. This opens up possibilities for it to be viewed as part of the organisational structure, not only of educational institutions, but of other organisations too. Much depends on the organisation's primary activity, and the extent to which career guidance in its different forms is viewed as necessary or useful for the support of this primary activity, as a valuable enrichment of it, or as marginal to it (Law, 1996a). The activities of 'managing' and of 'innovating/systems change' in the SCAGES list are designed to attend to such organisational issues.

The fourth distinction is *between reactive and proactive approaches*. Traditional matching approaches tended to take the opportunity structure as given, and to confine the role of guidance as fitting individuals into it. Counselling and careers education approaches have potentially viewed the individual in a more proactive role, but have been criticised for not paying sufficient attention to the limitations of the opportunity structure (Roberts, 1977). Educational guidance services for adults, however, introduced stronger proactive approaches, based on the premise that the needs and interests of learners should take precedence over those of educational providers; hence the inclusion in both the UDACE and SCAGES lists of enabling individuals in their dealings with providers, advocating on their behalf, and feeding back information on unmet needs (see Oakeshott, 1990). Such activities are likely to be more constrained in relation to occupational opportunities, where the notion of designing opportunities in response to individual needs and interests is likely to be given less legitimacy. Nonetheless, the feedback role of the Careers Service in relation to the design of government-funded youth training schemes has at times received formal recognition, and one of the arguments for locating career guidance within work organisations is that it can support a more dynamic social–exchange process between individuals and organisations, to the benefit of both (Kidd, 1996).

The final distinction is *between guidance and placement*. In the UDACE and SCAGES lists, the nearest activity to placement is 'enabling', defined by SCAGES as "supporting learners in dealing with agencies providing or influencing learning/employment opportunities", an example being "helping learners with making applications" (p 37). An earlier definition of 'enabling' more explicitly included the placement work conducted by the Careers Service and by university careers services, defined as "informing people about specific jobs and helping them to apply for them" (Watts, 1980, p 195). Some UK guidance services, however, do not undertake placement work of this kind, and in some countries placement is clearly separated from the guidance process and conducted by separate agencies (Watts et al, 1993). This is based on the view that placement activities are incompatible with guidance because they attend at least as much to the needs of opportunity providers as to the needs of individuals; they are, in essence, *brokerage* activities, whereas guidance is *individual-centred*. The tension is most evident where the placement operation includes a strong pre–selection filtering process, which can be viewed as a 'gatekeeper' function that can restrict the opportunities open to particular individuals. Some guidance services that include placement accordingly adopt a weaker form of it, in which they make available information on vacancies and leave individuals to apply where they wish, only seeking to influence such decisions through the general guidance process.

Levels of guidance provision

Guidance services operate at two main levels. As a basic level, they provide information about the spectrum of opportunities in terms of courses and jobs available to individuals. This can be a passive process, organised through publication of handbooks and information sheets and user-accessed computer databases, or a more active process, in which guidance professionals assist individuals to understand the variety of opportunities available so that they are in a position to choose between them. In either case, a costly data-gathering exercise has to be carried out by the organisations and professionals involved to collate and organise the information in a useful and usable way. The provision of information is clearly an essential precondition for effective and sensible choices to be made by individuals selecting a career path. It is difficult to imagine progress in the development of a learning society without a well-organised network of information points accessible to the various social groups that the learning society is supposed to encompass.

Beyond this, guidance services of a more sophisticated type come into play, covering a variety of activities. These may include provision of advice, training in job search skills, work orientation and confidence building, counselling to enhance individuals' awareness of their preferences, skills assessments to provide an individual insight into hidden and informal as well as formal qualifications and needs, and psychometric testing to uncover hidden preferences, interests and abilities. Psychometric testing is carried out by professionals with a range of skills and qualifications. In France, for example, professionals employed in the state-organised guidance services are required to hold a degree in psychology, whereas in the Netherlands, tests are now sold to individuals who may have had minimal training and may not be a member of a professional association.

We will argue in this book that both of these levels of services are essential components of an effective learning society. In this, we concur with views of Sir Christopher Ball, who, in his introduction to a Royal Society of Arts report argued that:

> The availability of high quality careers education and guidance for all throughout life is one of the prerequisites of the development of a world-class workforce and economic recovery in the UK. (Ball, 1993, p 4)

In other words, the provision of effective career guidance is a necessary condition for the creation of a learning society in which workers are continuously upgrading their skills, and making flexible changes to their career paths in response to rapidly fluctuating labour-market needs. Without some guidance to take individuals through the complexities of the educational and vocational choices that they face, such flexibility and responsiveness would be much diminished.

This is a somewhat contentious claim. After all, it might be argued that individuals do not need guidance to make the multiple transitions between education, training, unemployment and work. Individuals may be capable of making their own decisions about which course to take or which opportunities to pursue, and gathering and processing the information needed to make those decisions, without the assistance of professional guidance workers. However, the complexities of the training and labour markets in the learning society are such that exclusive reliance on self-help in the choice processes involved is insufficient. Access to properly organised guidance services is a fundamental element of the learning society.

Do guidance services provide real benefits to society?

To explore this claim further, it is helpful to distinguish between educational and vocational guidance.

Educational guidance has a direct bearing on the development of the learning society, by assisting individuals to improve their choices of education and training activities in which to invest their time, money and energy. It can thus help to reduce the drop-out rates from education and training courses (Killeen et al, 1992). A report by ECCTIS 2000 (1998) revealed that many students attending undergraduate courses at UK universities made poor choices of degree subjects, over one fifth of second-year students wishing they had chosen a different course of study. Improved educational guidance services are needed to assist individuals make better choices between the variety of courses on offer, taking into account the career opportunities to which they might lead. They should therefore help to increase the returns to investment in human capital. There may also be important external effects, spilling over from improved individual choices on to others in the educational process. For example, where drop-out rates from a course are high, the course may close down, adversely affecting the learning experience of others. Even if disappointed students do not drop out of a course, their lack of commitment may damage the learning experience of other course participants, and the effectiveness of a course as a whole.

Vocational guidance impacts on the development of the learning society in so far as it deals with choices made on exit from education and training courses. In order that the benefits of education and training can be maximised, it is necessary that the length of time to secure the next step taken on exit from courses should be minimised. This is both to reduce unemployment and also to avoid the depreciation of learnt skills that can occur if the duration of post-training unemployment is too lengthy. Effective vocational guidance reduces search costs to job seekers by providing them with information and advice about career paths and vacancies. By enhancing the process of job search, vocational guidance can reduce the frictional unemployment that is associated with mismatch between job offers and the supply of labour (Killeen et al, 1992).

The effective matching of individuals to jobs may also have implications beyond the direct effects of reducing frictional unemployment. By improving the matching of individuals to jobs, work satisfaction may be increased, with positive effects on productivity levels and on rates of job turnover. As a result of reduced job-turnover rates, employers' recruitment costs may be reduced. In addition to the external effects on employers' recruitment costs, the increased productivity of well-placed employees may also spill over on to other workers in a work team, improving their productivity in turn and enhancing the benefits of any work-based training schemes that are provided.

National strategies for lifelong access to guidance

Given these potential benefits, we argue that consistent national strategies are required for lifelong access to guidance in support of lifelong career development for all. Such strategies might have three prongs: first, guidance as an integral part of all educational provision; second, guidance as an integral part of all employment provision; and third, continuous access to independent guidance from a neutral base (Watts, 1994a).

The concept of career guidance as an integral part of education has two facets. The first is the role of compulsory schooling in providing the foundations for lifelong career development. This attaches particular importance to career education integrated into the curriculum and designed to develop the skills, knowledge and attitudes that will enable students to make and implement career decisions both now and in the future. Then, within but also beyond compulsory schooling, all educational provision should provide regular opportunities for students to relate what they are learning to its applicability in the wider society and to their own future career development. This will have implications for the curriculum; it also requires tutorial support, plus specialist career counselling services. A particularly powerful movement in British education in recent years has been the introduction of regular recording of achievement and action planning (Law, 1996b). Students are regularly encouraged to review their learning experiences, inside and outside the formal curriculum, and to define the skills and competencies they are acquiring through these experiences; they are also encouraged to identify and review their long-term career goals, their short-term learning objectives, and ways of achieving these objectives. Through this means, they develop and apply the skills of managing their own learning and linking it to their wider career development.

Interestingly, the same kinds of processes are also increasingly being set up within employment, which is the second prong of the strategy. Employees, too, are being given regular opportunities to review where they are and where they are going. Many organisations have introduced appraisal systems in recent years; often they are experienced by individuals as informing the organisation's decisions *about* them – about performance-related pay, for example – rather than their own decisions relating to their self-development. But in a growing number of cases these systems are being explicitly designed to focus on such self-development. Other organisations prefer to set up a parallel system of development reviews. In addition, an increasing number of organisations are introducing other systems to support career development: career planning workshops, assessment centres, career resource centres, mentoring systems and the like (Kidd, 1996).

The potential advantages of career guidance within education and employment are two-fold. First, they have more continuous contact with the individuals based in their organisation, and so are able to deliver more substantial and sustained guidance than any external service could do. Second, they are likely to be in a stronger position to influence their organisation to alter its opportunity structures in response to individuals' needs and demands, as revealed through the guidance process (the 'feeding back' activity in Figure 1).

On the other hand, guidance within education and within employment also share common limitations. First, they do not cover everybody; many people spend significant parts of their lives outside education and employment structures – because they are unemployed, for example, or engaged in child-rearing. Second, guidance services within particular organisations do not usually have a sufficiently broad view of opportunities outside that organisation. And third, the organisation can have a vested interest in the outcomes of the individual's decision, which can make it difficult to provide guidance that is genuinely impartial. For example, schools are rewarded financially if their students stay on beyond the compulsory school-leaving age; this means that some tend to bias their guidance in favour of their own offerings rather than the opportunities available elsewhere (HMI, 1992). Employers, too, tend to be reluctant to encourage valued employees to explore opportunities in other organisations.

For these reasons, it is crucial that there should be access to the broader and more impartial perspective which a neutral career guidance service can provide. Moreover, since the EU became a single market, with free mobility of goods and labour, the service needs to inform and advise clients about opportunities throughout the EU. These and other implications of EU membership are the subject of our next chapter.

THREE

Learning societies in the European Union

Introduction

The EU has been considerably strengthened as a global economic region in recent years. This, potentially at least, has significant implications for adult guidance services within and between the member states. First, and most obviously, the creation of a single market widens, spatially, the terrain for which providers should have information about opportunities in employment and learning. Second, the remit of the European Commission (EC) was extended as part of the Maastricht Treaty of 1992 to develop education and training policies at the EU level; this led to a set of White Papers shaping policy approaches and the development of a particular vision of a 'learning society'. Finally, and following on from this, the EU's concern to develop its own model of a learning society has led to a range of programmes and initiatives, some of which have included resources to co-fund guidance activities as part of projects within member states.

The creation of the single market in 1992 removed the formal restrictions on the mobility of labour between the member states. This had repercussions for employers, in that it obliged them to recognise qualifications acquired in other countries. It meant that government employment services had to facilitate job seekers to find out about vacancies not simply within the locality, region or country, but, technically, anywhere within the EU. By the same token, it implied that guidance services should be able to inform and advise clients about opportunities in the education and training markets anywhere within the single market. This clearly had ramifications for how adult guidance services should operate. It meant that providers needed more sophisticated methods of accessing, storing and retrieving data on an EU basis and that service providers would need to improve their networking mechanisms across member-state boundaries.

Despite the formal creation of the single market, numerous barriers remain in place which obstruct the real development of a unified education and employment space within the EU. In addition to the more or less hidden barriers linked to differences in national customs, languages and administrative systems, a key problem has been the difficulty in putting in place the required provision of EU-wide information, advice and guidance to the citizens of Europe about the opportunities available in the different EU countries. This lack of integration of the labour market has been reflected in high levels of unemployment and low levels of labour-market activity in the member states. Thus, in the late 1990s and the year 2000, a major feature of the European labour market was its low economic activity rate compared with the US and Japan. The activity rate in the EU has declined from 65.5% in 1973 to 60.5% in 1997 (EC, 1999c, p 7). Twenty years ago, activity rates in Europe and the US were broadly similar; now there are 14 percentage points between them – calculated by the EC as "equivalent to some 34 million jobs" (EC, 1999c, p 7). Male rates of activity are similar, but activity rates for young people, 'prime age' women and older people tend to be lower in Europe. A second feature of the turn of century European labour market is sustained high levels of unemployment. Women tend to have higher rates of unemployment than men in nearly all the member states (one of the exceptions is the UK) (see Rubery et al, 1999). The EU has developed policies to enhance economic growth and competitiveness, putting an emphasis on enhancing activity rates and combating unemployment.

The Maastricht Treaty extended the competency of the EC with regard to education and training policies. It allowed the Commission to develop policies to complement the actions of the member states in these fields. Two crucial White Papers were produced in the mid-1990s, which shaped the EU's approach to economic (EC, 1994a) and social policy (EC, 1994b). They focused on the twin goals of developing economic competitiveness and avoiding social exclusion. A third White Paper laid the foundation for creating a European learning society (EC, 1996a). There is an assumption in these White Papers that, provided the unemployed – and indeed employees – develop their skills, jobs will follow. Skill deficits are seen as inhibiting economic growth. There is a tension, however, between policies that are designed to address the goal of economic competitiveness on the one hand and those that might be appropriate for the avoidance of social exclusion on the other. This tension has ramifications for the focus and delivery of guidance services.

The White Papers and follow-up activities have influenced the design and reform of EC co-funded action programmes. While there is an acknowledgement of the importance of guidance in the White Papers overall, the approach taken to its provision through the programmes is fragmentary. There is some reluctance on the part of the Commission to define or restrict activities undertaken in the name of guidance, largely as a result of the principle of subsidiarity, which abrogates responsibility to the most appropriate level of governance. Nevertheless, guidance services are identified as an essential component of policies and programmes designed to foster mobility and enhance skills and employability, all of which are seen as integral to the goal of economic competitiveness. Hence the inclusion of guidance as an activity for which co-funding can be provided. However, the availability of co-funding has itself had an impact on the focus and direction of some services within member states. The extent to which EU co-funding is sought, and its significance in the income stream of providers, varies considerably, both by member state and by the sector of the provider. Institutional arrangements are crucial in determining the role of EC co-funding at the local level.

This chapter begins with a review of the history of the EC's role in supporting guidance in the member states, examining in particular the implications of the single market for guidance services. It gives an account of the EU-level framework of policies and programmes. It then explores the significance of institutional arrangements for the extent to which services within member states respond to them.

Historical context to EU policy on guidance

The EC first established guidelines for a vocational training policy in 1963. These included a commitment to guidance for young people and adults. This was followed up with a *Recommendation* on 24 August 1966 advocating that member states should promote vocational guidance. While a *Recommendation* does not have the force of law, it does provide a strong message to member states.

In terms of the Commission's own activities, guidance for young people was an element of two Community Action Programmes on the Transition from School to Working Life from 1978 to 1987, known as the Transition Programmes (for an account of these programmes, see IFAPLAN, 1987). The EC also commissioned a series of reports describing guidance provision within the individual member states to encourage greater familiarity across boundaries. A report by Watts et al (1988) provided one of the first comparative studies across the EU. It focused on the changing role of professional guidance services and the linkages between them for those aged 14 to 25. The report noted three major trends:

- a view of guidance as a continuous process throughout life;
- a move towards a more open, professional model;
- an emphasis on the individual as an active agent in the guidance process.

An updated version of this report was subsequently published which included a review of guidance services for adults (Watts et al, 1993). The authors argued that educational and vocational guidance services have a crucial role to play in fostering efficiency and social equity in access to educational and vocational opportunities. The trends in the previous report were confirmed and a fourth trend noted:

- more awareness of the European dimension on guidance provision, in particular an increased emphasis on the implications of the single market.

In addition, the EC and its member states are supporting cooperation between the 5,000 public employment service offices in the EU as part of the European Employment Strategy, agreed at the Amsterdam and Luxembourg summits in 1997. The provision of modern and efficient employment services is recognised as being crucial by the Commission (EC, 1999a, p 14). Hence, for public employment services, over a relatively short space of time, there has been a shift from working in relative isolation, through a growing need to know about approaches to guidance in other member states, to an increasing imperative to begin working across national boundaries.

The creation of the single market in 1992, which led to the removal of restrictions on the mobility of labour within the EU, had considerable implications, in theory at least, for the spatial dimension of information and advice which guidance services are now called upon to provide (Banks et al, 1990; Watts, 1992). While the extent of human mobility may be rather less developed than anticipated in some quarters (see Field, 1997), nevertheless job seekers are technically able to choose between vacancies anywhere within the EU. Hence, there is an onus of responsibility on those working in locally-based employment services to make available information about opportunities on an EU–wide basis, not just for employment but for education and training opportunities too. Moreover, as Watts et al (1993, p v) describe, there is a growing awareness among guidance providers of the implications of the single market for:

- the mobility of labour;
- employers' need for staff able to operate in more than one culture and language;
- the development of a European dimension in the work of a growing number of workers.

Members of EURES, the European network of employment services, are exploring methods of tackling this ambitious project on behalf of job seekers and employers. EURES comprises the public employment services of all the member states, plus those of Norway and Iceland, along with regional and national bodies concerned with employment, as well as other institutions interested in labour mobility (including the EC itself). It exists principally "to inform, advise and assist European citizens who want to work in another country and employers who want to recruit abroad" (EC, 1999a, p 15).

One of the major developments in the late 1990s to impinge on the work of the employment services has been the technical capacity to set up very large computerised databases which can be accessed at the local level. This is particularly significant for storing and retrieving information about the EU labour market. As part of the activities of EURES, a computerised databank of jobs and a living and working conditions databank have been compiled (EC, 1994b). Similarly, EU-wide computerised databases have been developed listing education and training courses, to which members of the general public have access through their respective local public employment services office. The EURES Internet site provides access to the national sites of public employment services as well as to the EURES jobs databank and information about moving to study, train or work in another member state. There is a growing market in such databases; many private companies are developing them, together with software to sell to a range of bodies that include guidance among their activities.

While the issue of provision of information may be addressed through such databases, it clearly needs expertise to advise clients on opportunities they find listed within them. One initiative to address this has been the establishment of a core network of about 500 'Euroadvisers' throughout the EU, trained specifically to deal with transnational job seekers and job providers (EC, 1994b, pp 37-8, 1999a, p 15). Closer links between guidance professionals in higher education have been facilitated by the

Forum Européen de l'Orientation Académique (FEDORA), set up in 1988; this has produced a comparative review of higher education guidance and counselling services across the member states (Watts and Van Esbroeck, 1998). Regular European-wide conferences are now held on the use of computers in careers guidance (see NCGE, 1997).

There is some evidence of concern from the EC that employment services should work more closely together and of this beginning to happen. A Commission communication published in 1999 invites the member states, the Social Partners and the public employment services to take 'concerted action' (EC, 1999b). A joint mission statement for the public employment services, published in the same year, describes their tasks, aims and strategies to achieve them. The public employment services have also developed a 'memorandum of understanding' for the development of the EURES network (EC, 1999b).

Hence the net effect of the single market on guidance services in the member states has been to encourage transnational cooperation between public employment service providers, which include guidance professionals, and to provide an additional imperative for the computerisation of information. Despite these advances, it remains difficult to assess precisely the EC's approach towards guidance policy, save to say that networking and a better information base are clearly regarded as essential to the single market. The next section examines the White Papers that have been shaping EU policy and programmes, picking out implications for guidance provision.

The White Papers on economic, social, and teaching and learning policy

During the mid-1990s, the EC produced three White Papers which, combined with the provisions of the Social Chapter and the agreements reached on the new Treaty at the June 1997 Amsterdam Summit, set the framework for policy making at the EU level well into the 21st century. The first White Paper was on economic policy: *Growth, competitiveness, employment: The challenges and ways forward into the 21st century* (EC, 1994a). The second was on social policy: *European social policy: A way forward for the Union* (EC, 1994b). The third was on teaching and learning: *Teaching and learning: Towards the learning society* (EC, 1996a).

The key element of these policy documents is a twin concern with fostering economic competitiveness and the avoidance of 'social exclusion' (Rees, 1998a). The notion of a learning society is a central plank in both these objectives. Improving the skills of the workforce through vocational education and training is identified as crucial to the development of the economic competitiveness of the single market (Rainbird, 1993). This fits the first of our models of the learning society; skills are identified as important for economic growth.

In the economic White Paper (CEC, 1994a), active labour-market policies are promoted. These are described elsewhere as principally being training (which accounts for about 30% of expenditure on such policies in the EU), work experience and job search assistance, including guidance (CEC, 1996; Ducatel et al, 2000). Of these, job search assistance with a guidance component has been identified as the lowest cost active labour- market policy and the most effective (OECD, 1996). In the White Paper, active labour-market policies are specifically described in terms of creating a better match between labour supply and demand through developing closer liaisons with undertakings or by the establishment of private employment agencies. New, more labour intensive service activities are advocated, which might suggest underpinning the second of our models of the learning society (personal development), although the discourse is couched very firmly in terms of 'encouraging people to work'. The White Paper also discusses one of the major concerns of member states – the cost of welfare – and advocates an examination of social protection systems to target benefits to those most in need (EC, 1994a, pp 140-1).

Skill development is also seen as essential in the social policy White Paper (EC, 1994b). This is in order to maximise the opportunities for the socially excluded to gain paid work. Some of the discussion of social exclusion is closer to the second model of a learning society we outlined in Chapter One, geared towards personal development and self-fulfilment. However, it is couched firmly in terms of an end result of enhancing human resources and reducing welfare costs. As Levitas (1996) observes, the socially excluded are defined wholly in terms of their exclusion from the working labour force. The role of EURES is described in the social policy White Paper as a "forum for discussion of European employment issues at the operational level" (p 38), but this is exclusively in terms of its remit "to inform, counsel and place job seekers" (EC, 1994b). This suggests a dominant model still geared very closely to guidance as a brokerage service.

The third White Paper (EC, 1996a) is the one most focused on the development of a learning society. Here again, the model of a learning society is linked clearly to skill development. An appropriate guidance service is envisaged as one that promotes open access to information and guidance, servicing individuals' aptitudes and needs (EC, 1996a, p 34). The observation is made in the White Paper that the citizen of Europe has more information available to assist the process of selecting hotels and restaurants than choosing learning opportunities. It is emphasised that we need to know how occupations will develop and what skills will be needed in the future at the European level. The White Paper appears to be based on the belief that better information about learning and job opportunities will automatically lead to the enhancement of skills and thus improve the economic efficiency of the labour market. However, it is also stated that "social origins continue to *condition choices* made by individuals which can work against their social advancement" (EC, 1996a, p 35; our emphasis). This concern about the influence of social attributes on choice indicates an acknowledgement of the social construction of learning and labour markets.

Individuals' choices are indeed influenced to a greater or lesser extent by an awareness of the role of gender, race and other discriminators in the organisation of the labour market. The emphasis in Commission documentation on well-informed choices understates the effect of these factors. Nevertheless, the operation of social features in the allocation of positions in the labour market is acknowledged in that people with certain characteristics are identified as belonging to 'disadvantaged groups'; these are then targeted in social policy. The causes of group disadvantage are not addressed.

The EC's position on guidance can therefore be described as having both economic efficiency and social equity objectives. The vision of the learning society underlying these policies appears to correspond to the skills growth model, although there is some room for the personal development model too, if only in order to deliver the first more effectively. Both these models rely on the creation of effective, formal guidance services to deliver their goals. This is reflected in the approach taken by the EC to funding guidance activities in the member states.

EC co-funding for guidance

The main route through which the EC supports activities and projects is through the Structural Funds. Regions of the member states set their own priorities in accordance with national priorities, set within a framework agreed at EU level. Resources for guidance can be accessed through training and employment projects in Objective 1 areas (promoting regions lagging behind), Objective 2 areas (regions affected by industrial decline) or Objective 3 areas (combating unemployment and facilitating the integration of young people). The Commission also funds Action Programmes and Community Initiatives targeting either specific issues or groups it identifies as needing special attention. The programmes and initiatives have been described as 'laboratories' for the development of new approaches. Here, too, financial support for guidance activities has been provided by the Commission, although always as part of a project whose main focus has been on employment or training.

Medium Term Action Programmes on Equal Treatment for Men and Women

One of the areas where guidance work has been supported by the EC has been through a series of Medium Term Action Programmes on Equal Treatment for Men and Women, a positive action measure to assist women in employment. Equal treatment was a principle enshrined in the 1957 Treaty of Rome, which set up the forerunner to the EU, the European Economic Community. However, the principle was largely ignored until the 1970s, when an Equal Opportunities Unit was set up in the Employment Directorate (formerly DG V) and a series of Directives was issued. These Directives obliged member states to introduce their own equal-pay and sex-discrimination legislation where it did not already exist. While necessary, such legislation has proved a blunt instrument for challenging the rigidities of patterns of gender segregation in education, training and the labour market and for combating the pay gap between men and women. It was in recognition of this that the Commission introduced the Medium Term Action Programmes on Equal Treatment for Men and Women to support projects designed to bring women's skills up to the level of men's (Rees, 1998b). The first Medium Term Action Programme ran from 1982 to 1985 and was followed by three further Programmes. Plans are under way for a fifth. The Programmes support training and employment projects especially aimed at women, to assist them in entering work, in particular non-traditional areas of work, or in setting up their own businesses (Rees, 1998b). Supplementary activities include job preparation, confidence building, practice job interviews, work tasters and guidance. These measures have supported a range of third-sector organisations offering training and guidance for women throughout the EU.

More recently, the EU has extended its equal-treatment approach to a range of other equality dimensions. In the Amsterdam summit, there was a commitment to extend the principle of equal treatment to people on the grounds of disability, ethnic origin and race, religious belief, sexual orientation and age. This endorses growing concerns about the 'social exclusion' of such groups, although the nature of their exclusion is not clearly articulated. The legitimacy of positive action measures for women was underlined in the new Treaty, and gender mainstreaming is identified as the major Commission policy approach to gender equality in the future – that is, integrating equal opportunities for women and men into all Community policies, programmes and actions. This contrasts with the more passive approach of informed choice in the labour and learning markets, supplemented by special treatment of disadvantaged groups, which underpins the three White Papers.

Action programmes on vocational education and training

A number of vocational education and training action programmes designed to address concerns about the development of human resources were set up in the 1980s by the Education, Training and Youth Directorate (formerly DG XXII, now the Education and Culture Directorate). They were intended to focus on key issues and special groups (see Rees, 1998b). The first to include a significant guidance element was the PETRA Action Programme that ran from 1988 until 1995 and concentrated on vocational training for young people and their preparation for adult and working life. Under its auspices, a network of national information centres on guidance for young people was set up, and a *European handbook for guidance counsellors* was produced (EC, 1994c). In 1995, the Action Programmes on education and training (including PETRA) came to an end and were superseded in the following year by two broader programmes: SOCRATES, an Action Programme on education, and LEONARDO DA VINCI, an Action Programme on training. Many of the foci of previous programmes were included in these new ones. Both include elements for guidance activities, including guidance for adults. Moreover, the national information centres were sustained under LEONARDO DA VINCI. A second phase for the two Action Programmes was launched in January 2000.

Community initiatives

There are currently 13 Community initiatives supported by money from the European Social Fund (ESF). In the late 1990s, guidance activities were most likely to be supported in projects under two such initiatives: EMPLOYMENT, which targets disadvantaged groups, and ADAPT, which is aimed at anticipating industrial change and dealing with its effects – in essence, targeting those at risk of redundancy. Both are now to be superseded by a new Community initiative, EQUAL. EMPLOYMENT has comprised 6,080 projects aimed at people identified as having 'particular difficulties' in the labour market, organised under four strands:

- INTEGRA – the most disadvantaged, already 'excluded' or at risk of 'exclusion' from the labour market;
- HORIZON – people with disabilities;
- YOUTHSTART – young people without qualifications;
- NOW – women.

Support for guidance within ADAPT and these last three strands of EMPLOYMENT was described by the Commission in the terms shown in Figure 2 (EC, 1995, pp 10–11).

These are broad, permissive definitions rather than specifications. They do not have precise implications for who should provide guidance, or for whether they should be professionally qualified or a member of a professional body. Through projects co-funded by the EC via any of these programmes and initiatives, a range of public, private and third-sector organisations are accessing resources to support projects that

Figure 2: European Commission Community initiatives

ADAPT	development and reinforcement of guidance and counselling services (within the framework of industrial restructuring)
NOW	(New Opportunities for Women) assistance for the creation or development of guidance/counselling and training services for women
HORIZON	support for the creation of personalised counselling services and setting up reception/guidance service centres for people who are handicapped and/or threatened with exclusion
YOUTHSTART	definition of objectives and standards in the field of vocational guidance for young people in difficulty

include a guidance component. However, under each programme and strand, co-funding is only available for adult guidance as part of other activities, such as education, training, enterprise support, exchanges, and employment projects. Adult guidance tends to be a minor part of the activity concerned. In some member states, those providing guidance in projects supported by these programmes are people who are not necessarily professionally trained. They are more likely to be primarily educators, trainers or community development workers.

Moreover, what is provided under the name of guidance varies widely, from provision of information, through group-work preparation for returning to work, to in-depth counselling. The growing significance of third-sector providers targeting groups identified as disadvantaged in (or socially excluded from) the labour market emerged as a significant factor in some of our case-study countries. Many were highly dependent on European co-funding, using it to lever resources from national, regional or local authorities.

Hence, overall EU support for guidance activities is closely linked to the funding of education, training and employment programmes and to positive action for women. This has impacted on the nature and provision of guidance services in individual countries. The Commission steps back from defining what guidance should entail; this is seen as the business of the member states.

Projects and exchanges funded under the Action Programmes are transnational, allowing social partners, students and lecturers, trainers and trainees to visit and work with their partner organisations in other member states. While the EC has put some emphasis on the need for guidance within these activities, it has not specified its nature or duration. The net effect is to provide some underpinning for guidance activities and to provide resources for a range of organisations involved in their delivery.

National action plans on employment

In order to ensure practical action to tackle the issues raised in the *Growth, competitiveness, employment* White Paper (EC, 1994a), and the commitment to putting employment at the centre of Europe's policy agenda at the Amsterdam summit in July 1997, a Jobs summit was held in Luxembourg in November of that year. At this summit it was agreed to implement a European Employment Strategy (known as the

Luxembourg process). Member states were asked to prepare annual national action plans on four 'pillars' or areas of action:

- to increase the employability of job seekers;
- to develop a culture of entrepreneurship;
- to promote adaptability for growth and employment;
- to strengthen equal opportunities.

These action plans, in effect, have been little more than a restatement of existing policies rather than developing new approaches to enhancing competitiveness and tackling unemployment. There has been some criticism, too, that equal opportunities has not been adequately mainstreamed in the other three pillars. Nevertheless, employment was confirmed as the top priority for the EU in 1999 (EC, 1999a) and the main policy principles included a shift from passive to active labour-market policies that include guidance.

In order to support member states' efforts, the EC has worked with the 5,000 local employment offices in the EU to assist them in developing common goals. During 1998, the EC adopted a Communication on public employment services that set out five main areas of work (EC, 1999a):

- public employment services should be informed of as many vacancies as possible;
- there should be arrangements to ensure systematic case management of every registered unemployed job seeker;
- public employment services should contribute to the coordinated delivery of all services to job seekers;
- public employment services should be used to facilitate international labour mobility;
- strong partnerships should be developed with all key players in the labour market.

The confirmation of employment as the main goal of the EU, and the development of national action plans complemented by EU-level policies and actions such as the ESF to support the member states' plans, secure the emphasis at EU level on the skills growth model of the learning society. This implies an emphasis on job brokering as the main activity of guidance services.

Institutional arrangements favouring EC co-funding

For careers services and other private-sector or third-sector providers of guidance services, certain institutional arrangements are more effective than others for securing access to EC co-funding for guidance services. First of all, it is clearly helpful to be operating in an area that is eligible for Structural Funds (such as a declining region or area of high unemployment). However, services operating anywhere within the EU and in eligible countries can apply for funding under the Action Programmes. Second, the political will to support EC co-funded activities must be there. This is essential to lever matched funding from other sources. Third, it is necessary to make an investment in acquiring cultural capital in the ways of the Commission. This can be achieved through, for example, the offices of regional governments, consortia offices based in Brussels, the use of consultants or growing in-house expertise. This assists in being aware of and able to prepare for calls for tender before they are published, cracking the jargon of the EC, understanding the text between the lines, and providing the appropriate answers to score maximum points when filling in the forms. Fourth, having appropriate working partners in place from which partnerships for bids can be developed, both in the bidding area and transnationally, is vital. Fifth, effective organisational infrastructure is important to accommodate the heavy bureaucratic and financial demands of EC co-funding. Finally, in order to secure funding specifically for adult guidance, projects need to embed it into other activities such as training, preparation for work, employment projects, and so on.

Some member states and some regions and localities within them are much more active than others in making applications and securing EC co-funding for adult guidance. There is an opportunity cost to be calculated; to what extent does the activity for which EC co-funding is available map on to local needs and agendas? There is also a threshold below which the bureaucracy surrounding EC co-funding is not cost-effective. For some providers, the calculations have led to their ignoring the EC as a source of support for adult guidance.

Moreover, the use made of European co-funding through Action Programmes and Community initiatives has highlighted cultural differences in the conceptualisation of 'guidance' (see Chapter Two; also Rees et al, 1999). Indeed, it is through the diversity of approaches to guidance activities co-funded by the EU that we can trace differences among and within member states in the modelling of a learning society and in the treatment of 'disadvantaged groups'. These issues are explored through our case studies, in particular in the UK and in the Netherlands (see Chapters Five and Seven).

Conclusion

The focus of this chapter has been on adult guidance in the context of the EU approach to a learning society. In the context of the single market, there are some tensions and confusions at the European level between who should be responsible for information provision as opposed to in-depth guidance provision. There is also a potential contradiction between developing provision strategically to develop an economically competitive 'learning society', and targeting services at the disadvantaged or 'socially excluded'. The net effect of this dual aim is a diverse range of institutional patterns of provision in the member states. This ensures an increasingly varied access to different kinds of adult guidance services from a wide range of providers, as part of a disparate set of activities, as we shall see from the international comparisons in the next section.

Part Two
International comparisons

FOUR

United Kingdom

Introduction

This chapter describes the development of adult guidance services in the UK up to the present day. It begins with an account of the historical evolution of career guidance services, with particular attention to the development of the Careers Service. It charts the process of marketising careers services in the mid–1990s which, although mainly concerned with guidance for young people, had major implications for the provision of adult guidance. It thus provides the background context to the local case studies described in Chapter Five. Following the change of government in 1997, there have been further rapid developments in the field of guidance and guidance-related activities; these too are documented briefly in this chapter. The final section looks at the growing divergence in institutional arrangements in the UK following the devolution that took place in 1999.

The evolution of career guidance services in the UK

Career guidance services were creatures of late industrialisation. Traditionally, the allocation of work roles was determined largely by the family and surrounding networks into which one was born. With industrialisation, however, the division of labour eventually extended to a point where such traditional mechanisms of role allocation became insufficient, and formal guidance services were developed to supplement them.

It was accordingly at the end of the 19th century and during the early years of the 20th century that the first vocational guidance services began to appear both in the USA and in Europe (Keller and Viteles, 1937; Brewer, 1942). In the UK, the early services were focused exclusively towards young people, and were strongly placement-oriented; their concern was to help young people to make the transition to work. Following the Second World War, these juvenile employment officers were merged into a national Youth Employment Service, embracing young people up to the age of 18, with central government providing the service if local authorities chose not to do so. The service had responsibility not only for guidance and placement but also for the administration of unemployment benefits to young people (Heginbotham, 1951; Killeen and Kidd, 1996).

Meanwhile, limited services began to appear within universities and schools. The origins of university appointment boards can be traced back to 1892; by the mid-1950s all universities had such a service, offering advisory interviews, information about careers, employers and jobs, and placement activities (University Grants Committee, 1964). In schools, careers teachers were mentioned from the late 1920s, and by the 1960s were being widely appointed; their tasks included managing information and providing facilities and support for the work of the youth employment officer (Daws, 1972). In colleges of further education, guidance services appeared more slowly, mainly because it was assumed that students had already made a vocational commitment prior to entry (Marks, 1975).

It was in the 1960s and early 1970s that guidance services began to develop in a more rapid and extensive way. The growth of educational and vocational options extended the range of choice for many young people, and increased the demand for help in making such choices. The 1973 Employment and Training Act transformed the Youth Employment Service into a Careers Service, and made it a statutory duty for local education authorities (LEAs) to provide such a service. Responsibility for the administration of unemployment benefit was removed. Subsequently, recognition was given in a Memorandum of Guidance to the provision of guidance "at appropriate stages during ... educational life", signalling a move away from a focus on the single point of transition to work. Youth employment officers were renamed careers officers, and required to complete an approved full-time training course (Killeen and Kidd, 1996).

Alongside the professionalisation of the Careers Service, two further significant developments occurred. The first was the emergence within schools, colleges and universities of the concept of 'careers education', as part of the curriculum. This was linked to the growth of interest in approaches focused on helping students to take responsibility for their decisions, rather than being passively dependent on the advice of experts. Schools began to establish classroom programmes designed to develop pupils' self-awareness, opportunity awareness, and skills for making decisions and transitions. By 1973, two thirds of schools offered such programmes, although often for leavers only (DES, 1973). In further and higher education, similar concepts began to emerge, although growth was slower and more patchy (Watts, 1977; Stoney and Scott, 1984).

The second significant development was the emergence of career guidance services not only for young people, but also for adults. In 1966, an all-age Occupational Guidance Service was set up within the Department of Employment. The 1973 Employment and Training Act permitted, although it did not oblige or fund, LEA Careers Services to offer guidance to adults; a number took advantage of this opportunity. In addition, the first educational guidance service for adults started in Belfast in 1967, and by 1979 there were 15 such services in different parts of the UK (ACACE, 1979). A variety of other forms of adult guidance provision also began to develop, in the private, voluntary and public sectors (Watts, 1980).

The public-expenditure cuts of the late 1970s and 1980s saw the brake being applied to these developments. The Occupational Guidance Service was dismantled in 1980/81. Efforts to establish the LEA as the natural coordinating focus for networks of adult guidance providers (UDACE, 1986) faltered with the undermining and weakening of LEAs. The pressures on public expenditure made a funded extension of the Careers Service's statutory client-group ever less likely, particularly as guidance remained low on the public-policy agenda. Career guidance remained firmly established as part of social-welfare provision for young people, but within these terms was at risk of gradual erosion as a result of general political and economic pressures on the welfare state. It certainly seemed unlikely to attract the increased resources needed to extend the statutory entitlement to wider client groups.

In the late 1980s and early 1990s, however, guidance began to move up the public-policy agenda. The Confederation of British Industry (CBI) (1989) argued influentially that an improved careers education and guidance was one of the keys to achieving the skills revolution required for national economic competitiveness. Evidence was marshalled to indicate the economic as well as social benefits of career guidance provision (Killeen et al, 1992). Instead of being viewed as a rather marginal area of social welfare provision, guidance began to be viewed as a part of "that most politically acceptable of professions: the market-makers" (McNair, 1990, p 15); a means of making the labour market, and the emerging education and training market, operate more effectively.

During this period, under the Conservative government, market principles had been applied to many areas of the public sector (see

Chapter One). The next section examines in more detail the marketisation of the Careers Service that occurred in the mid–1990s.

The marketisation of the Careers Service

Traditionally the main vocational guidance provision for young people has been based around the Careers Service, run and managed at local level by LEAs (Killeen and Kidd, 1996). The statutory responsibility of these local career services has been to provide guidance to school pupils, school leavers, students in vocational part–time education, people under the age of 19 not in education or training, and people with special educational needs of any age to assist them in their choice of career. However, under the 1993 Trades Union Reform and Employment Rights Act, a fundamental change in the way careers services were organised and funded took place. As in other areas of public service, such as health, education and community care, there was an attempt to introduce market–type forces (quasi–markets) into the provision of the service. In the case of the Careers Service, this was to be achieved through a competition for the right to supply services in a particular locality ('contracting out'). Careers services were privatised and removed from LEA control, and funded on the basis of a contract specified directly with the state (in England, the Department for Education and Employment, through the regional Government Offices; in Scotland, the Scottish Office; in Wales, the Welsh Office).

The new providers retained a statutory duty to provide guidance services to school pupils as before, and these services were still to be provided free of charge at the point of delivery, paid for by the state through the contract. The core contract, which covered 85% of the budget, was funded by a capitation formula based on the number of school pupils in an area, augmented by a target-based element of funding covering the remaining 15%, which was linked to the number of action plans achieved with the client group. A system of competitive tendering for guidance contracts on an area basis was introduced. By 1997, all the LEA careers services had been converted to private companies or partnerships and contracted out. Most were converted into partnerships of LEAs and TECs/LECs. In a few cases, however, new service providers entered the field and the careers service established a separate identity from the TEC/LEC. Nearly all the new careers companies were set up as companies limited by guarantee, often with a non-profit status, although some were established as limited-liability shareholder companies or took other legal forms (Chatrik, 1997).

In a few areas, the careers services had established adult guidance services, funded and promoted by local authorities that saw an emerging need. However, in England and Wales, the main stimulus to the development of adult guidance services had come from the employer-led TECs (in Scotland, the LECs) established in the early 1990s (Hawthorn, 1996a). These organisations were made responsible for implementing the government's vocational training programmes on a decentralised local basis, and in so doing, were drawn into the provision of adult guidance services. TECs (which in 2001 will be replaced by locally-based Learning and Skills Councils – see below) typically bid for resources from various government programmes, normally channelled through the regional Government Offices. These programmes were in due course gathered together in the Single Regeneration Budget (SRB), and TECs competed for funds from this source, augmented in many cases by matched funding from the European Social Fund (ESF). In other cases, TECs bid directly to government departments for specific programme funds.

A survey conducted by the Institute of Careers Guidance (ICG) in 1995 revealed that by that time 86% of careers companies in Britain provided adult guidance services (ICG, 1996). Two important sources of funding in the 1990s were the Gateways to Learning programme (for unemployed adults) and the Skill Choice programme (for employed adults). In England and Wales, TECs typically contracted out adult guidance services to a range of providers within their locality who were in competition with one another for TEC funds. In this way, a quasi-market in adult guidance was established, based on a separation of the purchase and the provision of services. In some cases, the purchasing function in these quasi-markets was devolved to the users of the services through voucher schemes (in particular, under the Gateways to Learning and Skill Choice programmes). Elsewhere, the quasi-market was structured through contracting out to service providers who were funded either on a block-contract or a capitation basis.

Where new careers companies were organised as LEA/TEC (in Scotland, LEA/LEC) partnerships, the two main organisations providing adult guidance were brought together. In these cases, the TEC often provided direct block funding to the careers company to support the provision of adult guidance services. In effect, the competitive quasi-market in provision of services by TEC-funded providers was replaced by the prior competition for the contract to deliver the careers service.

In cases where an independent company won the careers service contract, this fusion did not take place, and the TEC continued to act as an independent purchaser of adult guidance services in the local quasi-market. These two models of provision that emerged following the implementation of the 1993 Act are clearly visible in the local case studies reported in Chapter Five.

A different approach to the provision of guidance services was adopted in Scotland. LECs received their funding through the Scottish Office (now the Scottish Executive). Rather than adopting competitive tendering for contracts, the Scottish Office chose to encourage local authorities and LECs to work together to bid for the careers service contract for their area. The Scottish Office had supported an initiative on adult guidance, the Adult Educational Guidance Initiative in Scotland (AEGIS). The strategy, developed in 1996, included an action plan on lifelong learning and guidance, a telephone helpline and database, a cross-sectoral guidance team and support for local guidance networks (see Connelly et al, 1998). Seventeen adult guidance networks were set up in 1997, with an initial budget of £1.2m for a three-year period. They were designed to coordinate activities and avoid duplication of effort. Learning Direct Scotland is a freephone service originally funded by the Scottish Office; it predated the setting up of Learning Direct (now Learndirect) in England (see below). It provides information, advice and guidance by qualified advisers on education and training opportunities, childcare and progression routes. For more in-depth guidance, callers are referred to the adult guidance network in their area. A Scottish Guidance Group has advised the Scottish Office (now Scottish Executive) inter alia on the training and development needs of adult guidance networks and on the development of quality.

The defining characteristic of quasi-market mechanisms is not privatisation per se, but marketisation, the attempt to mimic market mechanisms within a system of public ownership, or, where ownership is transferred to private or non-profit providers, through a system of regulation (Walsh, 1995). The privatised careers companies in the UK operate in both a quasi-market and a real market. As we have seen, a quasi-market was established by requiring the careers companies to compete for contracts for the right to deliver a service to the core statutory group of school pupils, school leavers and young adults in an educational environment, and in addition by encouraging many careers companies also to compete for further contracts to provide services to non-core clients (adults in specific situations: unemployed people, women returnees and so on). In addition, a real market has begun to emerge for adults, since the careers companies have the right to charge fees to their adult users for their services.

Careers services have 'mixed' contracts in that risks are shared between the purchaser and the provider. The contracts have a core block element but also some element of cost–per–case contracting, a variable element linked to the achievement of targets. A difficulty with targets is that they can tend to distort the allocation of effort of the provider in the direction of the target, and so reduce the productive efficiency of the organisation. The structural arrangements mean that careers companies may, for example, be tempted to discriminate against those clients with low employment prospects, or to concentrate on the core contract and decline to offer services to adults.

In their study of welfare–state reforms in the fields of health, housing, education and social care, Le Grand and Bartlett (1993) developed a number of evaluation criteria for measuring their success. These criteria can also be used to evaluate the success or otherwise of reforms in the field of career guidance. The criteria include measures of efficiency, responsiveness, choice and equity. The inclusion of measures of responsiveness and choice indicate that welfare–state reforms should be evaluated not only on narrow economic considerations of efficiency (although this is in itself a complex indicator), but also in terms of the extent to which users' needs are met in a broader social sense. In addition, equity considerations are of importance in any evaluation of welfare systems, particularly so since welfare services are often provided precisely in order to overcome adverse distributional effects of what may otherwise be efficient, market–determined economic transactions (such as in markets for labour, capital, land, and other goods and services).

In general, therefore, a number of conditions must be met if market–type reforms in the public sector are to achieve the desired results of improvements in efficiency, choice and responsiveness, while also taking equity criteria into account. These conditions include considerations about the market structure, information, transaction costs, uncertainty, motivation and cream–skimming. Briefly, these conditions state that:

- markets should be broadly competitive or at least contestable;
- there should be symmetric information between providers and purchasers (the agents or final users);
- transaction costs and the level of uncertainty over the level of future transactions should not be too great;
- providers should in most circumstances be motivated to make profits, or at least to respond favourably to financial incentives;

- the opportunities to engage in cream-skimming (ie to discriminate between users on the basis of cost) should be minimised.

In the case of the reforms of the statutory careers services for young people in the UK, the market structure conditions could have been met by competition at the bidding stage and so would have been effective to meet the desired efficiency conditions. But in at least 13 of the original 14 'pathfinder' contract competitions, only a single bidder entered the competition, usually the newly privatised careers service itself. However, as the system developed, more bidding competition began to emerge, with hostile takeovers occurring, and some expansionist, predatory, independent providers (such as Nord Anglia) assuming the role of significant players. In the case of monopoly market structures, Le Grand and Bartlett (1993) argue that second-best considerations suggest that the motivation condition should also be broken – that is, providers should not necessarily be profit-makers. In conditions of monopoly, profit-maximising providers may restrict output and lower quality. As a result, the goals of efficiency, responsiveness and choice may be better met by non-profit providers which have internalised some of the interests of user groups into their own decision-making criteria, and so may be less prone to take opportunistic advantage of the monopoly market position. Therefore, the presence of large numbers of non-profit providers such as the TEC/LEA partnerships appeared to offer some hope of providing an effective service.

However, in the key area of adult careers guidance, the reforms made little impact. There was little improvement in the area of responsiveness and choice, largely because the insistence on the application of real markets for guidance services (through fee-charging) resulted in little increase in what was already a limited and restricted range of provision. A number of experiments were carried out with the introduction of vouchers for careers guidance services; however, these proved to be unsuccessful. A study carried out by Coopers & Lybrand (1994) showed that there was little if any noticeable improvement in responsiveness and choice, as users made little effort to discriminate among providers through the use of their vouchers. At the same time, the transaction costs of the scheme were extremely high, due to the administrative costs of organising and distributing the vouchers. As a result of this experiment, the idea of using vouchers as a means of organising the market for career guidance services was effectively abandoned as a tool of policy.

Other providers of adult guidance

There are some similarities and some differences in the institutional map and sets of arrangements for the delivery of adult guidance across the constituent countries of the UK. Divergence has become more marked since devolution. Here we describe the main providers of adult guidance in the UK, especially in England and Scotland, where our case-study localities (described in the next chapter) are based. The account takes us up to 1997. It is followed by an account of changes since 1997, including some initial trends in the post-devolution era regarding the framework for adult guidance services in England, Scotland, Wales and Northern Ireland.

The Employment Service

The Employment Service (ES) is a UK-wide service and an Executive Agency of the Department for Education and Employment (DfEE) which is responsible for administering the Jobseeker's Allowance, giving information about vacancies to unemployed job seekers, and providing a recruitment service to employers. Its primary function is job placement, and each office is set targets for job placement rates to be achieved. There are additional targets based on certain categories – for example, for disabled people and for long-term unemployed people. Funding is provided through a core contract augmented by a variable amount related to achievement of targets.

The ES provides a limited range of guidance services. These are mainly oriented towards achieving job-placement targets, rather than providing guidance in the more general sense of promoting individual career development. In the mid-to-late 1990s, when our fieldwork was conducted, the first intervention took place when an unemployed person had failed to find work within a period of 13 weeks. It consisted of a programme called 'Job Search Plus' designed to provide help with training on CV writing and other job search skills. This training was externally contracted to private organisations or to the local TEC, giving a further example of quasi-market provision of adult guidance. After six months' unemployment, claimants went on to the 'Job Finder' programme, which involved interviews with ES advisers. This programme started early in 1997 and provided a series of interviews once a fortnight over a 14-week period. After 12 months of unemployment, there was further externally contracted provision called 'Job Plan', which comprised a one-week course, followed by interviews with advisers to consolidate it. After two years' unemployment, claimants went on to the Restart programme, which involved yet more courses.

One of the main routes through which the ES delivered adult guidance services was through a further scheme known as the 'Job Club', which was available to claimants who remained unemployed for over six months. The Job Club services were contracted to external providers including private companies, colleges, charities and, in some cases, the local careers service. The Job Club and other programmes gave training in job search skills, including formal sessions on interview techniques and CVs. They also provided labour-market information, including bringing in employers to talk about their businesses. All programmes included access to the 'Adult Directions' skills evaluation computer programme, and in some cases group leaders would refer people to local adult guidance providers.

In contrast to the careers service and the TECs and LECs, local ES offices traditionally have had little local autonomy, since external contracting is bound by Treasury guidelines. There is typically a regional list of preferred providers who are invited to tender for particular contracts for externally provided services and are then selected on criteria of value for money. A tender evaluation and scoring system is used to select and monitor the successful providers.

The private and voluntary sectors

It is often claimed that there is limited scope for the provision of guidance services on the private market (Watts, 1996b, 1999a; our interviewees). Nevertheless, there is a thriving private market in some areas of provision of adult guidance. The private sector has operated successfully in two main areas: first, in the provision of outplacement and redundancy services for companies undergoing restructuring; and second, through the work of recruitment agencies, which have an increasingly important role in brokering job placements in the flexible, part-time and temporary-contract labour markets. While the former group of private providers offers services in the mainstream of guidance (skills assessment, psychometric testing, job search skills training), the latter are more placement-driven. They offer only a peripheral range of guidance services as such, although they have increasingly been drawn into government-funded training programmes in collaboration with the TECs. The key point to note about both these sectors, however, is that the main source of funding is almost invariably through charges and fees to employers.

Alongside the private sector, a large number of guidance service providers have been established in the voluntary sector, often offering services to specific disadvantaged groups, particularly among ethnic minorities (see Jackson and Haughton, 1998). In many cases the growth of these voluntary-sector providers was stimulated by the quasi-market for guidance services organised and funded by the TECs. However, where the TEC-funded quasi-market was replaced by a LEA/TEC partnership, and this led to a redirection of TEC funds directly to the careers service to fund adult guidance provision, the role of the voluntary sector tended to diminish.

Further and higher education

Another key provider of adult guidance services is the further education (FE) and higher education (HE) sectors. These sectors are quite distinct from one another in terms of the nature and range of services that they provide. The FE sector was taken out of local authority control under the 1992 Further and Higher Education Act. Since then, funding has been channelled through the Further Education Funding Council (FEFC) in England, Scotland and Wales. FE colleges normally provide limited educational and vocational guidance, usually supplemented by services supplied by the local careers services which, under the 1973 Employment and Training Act, have been required to offer guidance services to full-time students and some part-time students in FE colleges (Hawthorn, 1996b). The largest element of guidance in colleges is 'entry guidance', which has been funded by the FEFC grant to colleges. However, this has tended to be geared towards promoting enrolment of individual students on college courses, and has sometimes been criticised on the grounds that there is little incentive to provide unbiased advice to prospective students. Nevertheless, this danger has been modified by the fact that part of the FEFC funding has also been linked to course completion rates and so the impact of potential bias may have been less than has sometimes been claimed (see Chapter Five).

The main problem with FE college guidance services is that they are severely restricted in scope. Most colleges provide only a limited service. In contrast, university careers offices tend to be better provided for, often with a substantial staff and a dedicated office or a separate building, although this varies considerably from university to university. Core funding typically comes from the university's own resources, but often there is also some input from employers, especially the larger corporations. Our case-study material provides ample evidence of the relatively favoured position of the HE sector, particularly in the older universities. A number of key issues for the HE sector were identified in a report by the National Institute for Careers Education and Counselling (NICEC) (Watts, 1997). One of the most important concerned the possibility of extending the scope of the HE guidance services to groups outside the immediate clientele of the university sector. Watts identified a number of possibilities, including continuing lifelong provision of services to all university students beyond graduation. One could also speculate whether it could be possible to open these university services to adult non-graduates, or to enhance the collaboration between the university sector and the adult guidance sector more generally. In other words, could town and gown collaborate in the provision of adult guidance services?

Other providers: the probation service and the armed forces

A range of other providers operates to deliver guidance services to particular special-needs groups. Prominent among these are the probation services, which are increasingly offering career guidance to ex-offenders. These initiatives are funded by the Home Office, which has acknowledged the link between the lack of employment opportunities for ex-offenders and the incidence of re-offending. As a result, a number of new initiatives are being sponsored, designed to promote the employability of ex-offenders and boost their employment prospects.

A second main area outside the mainstream is the provision of guidance services to retiring members of the armed forces. This area of work has been given greater prominence in recent years due to the end of the 'cold war' and the reaping of the peace dividend. The armed forces have been downsizing and retired military personal have unique problems in making the transition to civilian life. This requires special assistance from guidance professionals, which for some years was provided by a branch of the Regular Forces Employment Association. It received 80% of its funding from the Ministry of Defence (MoD) and 20% from various charities. The 'resettlement services' were run by the Tri-Service Resettlement organisation, which provided a range of guidance services depending on length of service, including how to write CVs, briefing on different industries, and in-depth guidance interviews. Retiring personnel also received a grant of £500 to do any 28-day course they chose in order to top up their skills – for example, a Heavy Goods Vehicle driving course or a business course. The whole of the Tri-Service Resettlement organisation was subsequently privatised and is now managed by Coutts Career Consultants, which won a competition between 160 companies that bid for the right to run the service.

New developments since 1997

Since the change of government in 1997, there have been a number of changes in policy affecting adult guidance. Some of the main ones will now be outlined.

New Deal

The 'New Labour' government introduced the New Deal in 1997 as a welfare-to-work strategy designed to shift the focus of the benefits systems from paying for unemployment to investing in the employability of the unemployed. It aims to help people find work and improve their prospects of remaining in sustained employment. Much of the discourse used to describe the New Deal is about combating social exclusion.

Within the New Deal, each entrant enters an initial 'Gateway' lasting up to three months. Advisory interviews focus on job search method, the identification of barriers to work, vocational guidance and training-needs assessment. If the unemployed person does not succeed in securing employment at the end of this period, it is followed by a three-month 'intense activity period' of mandatory activity and support and, if necessary, a further period of up to six advisory interviews and access to further career guidance.

The emphasis of this programme was initially on 18 to 25 year olds and lone parents; it was then extended to the long-term unemployed over 25 and, more recently, to job seekers aged 50 and over. A key element of the scheme is placing individuals who have been out of work with employers who receive a government subsidy. This is backed up by training through day release leading to National Vocational Qualifications (NVQs), together with options for full-time education. Employers are closely involved through a partnership approach. The programme has led to closer links between the ES and careers services.

In one small study of the New Deal, adult guidance professionals expressed concern that Gateway advisers have not been trained to nationally recognised standards in guidance (Irving and Barker, 1999). There are also equity issues, in that eligibility for the Jobseeker's Allowance is a qualifying criterion for participating in the New Deal; hence women not available to work full-time because of caring commitments are ineligible.

ConneXions

In relation to young people, social exclusion appears to have eclipsed the learning society as a focus of government concern. A new service for young people aged 13 to 19, ConneXions, will be launched in 2001, integrating the careers service with youth and other services. This new configuration will clearly have ramifications for adult guidance. The Careers Service as a separate entity is likely to disappear, being subsumed into the new arrangements. A more holistic approach is planned, with guidance for learning to work being brought together with advice and guidance on other personal and social issues, including, for example, drug dependency. Each young person will be allocated a 'personal adviser'. The scheme is being piloted in 2000 with a view to being implemented in tranches from April 2001. Watts and Sadler (2000) have identified a number of potential tensions in the proposed new arrangements, in particular regarding the arrangements for those young people still at school.

Learning and Skills Council

From 2001, the FEFC and the TECs are to be replaced by a Learning and Skills Council with responsibility for planning, funding and quality-assuring all post-16 education and training other than higher education. The national council will have two statutory committees – one for young people and one for adults – and there will also be 47 Local Learning and Skills Councils. This new configuration is expected to take the leading role in funding and planning of adult guidance, as well as being responsible for arrangements regarding the funding of guidance within post-16 education and training provision. There will be separate national arrangements in Wales. In Scotland, consultation is taking place on the Scottish Executive's paper *Opportunities and choice* (Scottish

Executive, 1999), a follow-up to the *Opportunity Scotland* White Paper that set out a strategy for lifelong learning (Scottish Office, 1998).

Information, Advice and Guidance for Adults (IAGA) Partnerships

The Learning and Skills Council will have responsibility for the new Information, Advice and Guidance for Adults (IAGA) Partnerships. £54m has been allocated over three years to set up these partnerships. Six 'pathfinder' areas were established in 1999/2000. There is a strong emphasis on quality in the new arrangements: providers who are members of the local partnerships must meet the Guidance Council's quality standards as a condition of funding. A new Guidance Accreditation Board (GAB) has been set up to implement these standards (Watts and Sadler, 2000).

Learndirect and Learning and Work Bank

Learndirect is a national telephone helpline and website providing free information and advice about learning opportunities. It is to be linked to an Internet-based Learning and Work Bank allowing enquirers to call up ES job vacancies and Learndirect's database of learning opportunities on-line. The first wave of Learndirect centres has been opened as a pilot scheme; up to 1,000 centres were scheduled to be opened by autumn 2000. Learndirect is part of the DfEE's University for Industry (UfI) initiative, a public–private partnership to stimulate demand for lifelong learning and improve access to learning. UfI has a target of providing information to 2.5 million people per year by 2002 and creating demand for one million courses and learning packages by 2004.

Individual Learning Accounts

The idea behind Individual Learning Accounts (ILAs), part of the government's lifelong learning strategy, is that individuals and employers will share with government the responsibility for investing in an individual's skills. There is scope for developing an important role for the funding of adult guidance in the ILAs (see Chapter Ten), although current political support for the scheme has been described as "fairly limited" (Watts and Sadler, 2000, p 9). ILAs are at present targeted at the employed.

Devolution

The provision of adult guidance services has always varied spatially according to the specifics of locally based arrangements. As a result of devolution, divergences are becoming accentuated among the constituent countries of the UK (see Watts, 1999b). The setting up of the Scottish Parliament and the National Assembly for Wales in 1999 has resulted in different foci in adult guidance apart from the statutory provision under the New Deal. The Northern Ireland Assembly, after its short-lived first session, is now operational again and new policies can be expected to emerge on guidance.

England

In England, an attempt is being made to develop a sustainable infrastructure for a new public service of information, advice and guidance for adults based on local partnerships arrangements. The partnerships are "initially being required to provide a free and universally available information and advice service on learning and work; the intention is to add in due course a guidance dimension, which may need to be charged for" (Watts, 1999b, p 2). This is intended to complement the Ufl's Learndirect helpline and website described above. The careers services are the lead partner in most areas.

Scotland

In Scotland, there has been a strong tradition of networks involved in the provision of adult guidance (see above). The Scottish Executive has extended the funding of the adult guidance networks until 2001, although it has not enhanced the size of the annual budget. The Scottish Guidance Group (set up by Scottish Office to develop a national approach to adult guidance) may remain as it is or it may become independent, able to represent the views of the guidance field to the Scottish Parliament. A current review of the careers services in Scotland (where provision of adult guidance varies) "may or may not lead in the direction of an all–age service" (Watts, 1999b, p 2). The careers services are likely to be the lead partner on adult guidance in many but not all areas. Learndirect in Scotland (which predated the launch of the service elsewhere) is delivered by UfI.

Wales

TECs have coordinated adult guidance networks for some years in Wales, supported through funding from the Welsh Office (now the National Assembly for Wales). These networks have provided free access to information and advice, and guidance for those not in work. Whereas in England, Scotland and Northern Ireland, Learndirect is being run by UfI, in Wales the Assembly has funded four regional centres to deliver the helpline and to develop links with adult guidance networks. Data are shared with Learndirect in England. The Assembly is also considering an all–age guidance service (Careers Wales) that would draw together the Careers Service, the Adult Guidance Initiative and Learndirect in each area (Watts, 1999b, p 3).

Northern Ireland

An all–age service is in effect delivered in Northern Ireland through the network of jobcentres managed by the Training and Employment Agency (T&EA). The T&EA operates the employment service and provides a careers service for young people and adults. The Department of Education for Northern Ireland (DENI) has drawn on support from the EU Special Support Programme for Peace and Reconciliation to invite a community organisation, the Educational Guidance Service for Adults (EGSA) in Belfast, to establish regional guidance networks through which impartial guidance provision will be available throughout Northern Ireland. An attempt is being made to bring the T&EA provision and educational guidance provision within a common framework.

Conclusion

Adult guidance services in the UK have had a complicated and fragmentary history. The marketisation of the Careers Service made a significant difference to the institutional arrangements for services for young people, which in turn had an impact on adult guidance services. There is a long list of players in the field, with different 'takes' on adult guidance. There are also spatial variations at the local level, and increasingly, as a consequence of devolution, different patterns are emerging in the constituent countries of the UK, in particular, trends towards or away from all-age guidance services.

Many of the new and planned initiatives in the field of adult guidance have been identified in the latter part of this chapter. It is too early to say how they will evolve. In-depth studies will be needed to assess their impact. Meanwhile, we will now examine the provision of adult guidance services in five case-study areas in the UK – four in England and one in Scotland – shortly after the beginning of the marketisation process. How did marketisation affect services for adults? How did the type of organisations that won the contract to deliver services for young people affect adult guidance services? Were there differences according to the state of the local labour market? These are some of the questions that we address in the next chapter.

FIVE

English and Scottish case studies

Introduction

This chapter reports on the findings of our in-depth research on the adult educational and vocational guidance systems in four localities in England and one in Scotland (see Appendix for details of the methodology). The main focus of the research is on the nature of the changes that took place following the marketisation of the Careers Service by the Conservative government in the mid-1990s. The LEA Careers Service was contracted out to new independent careers companies, many of which were made up of partnerships of the LEA and the local TEC. The chapter outlines the basis for selection of the case studies and describes their key features. Points of comparison are then drawn out, focusing on key elements of the marketisation process: funding, access and equity.

Four English localities were selected, together with one in Scotland. The case studies were selected on the basis of two main criteria:

- the type of careers company that had been established;
- the degree of tightness in the local labour market.

The first criterion was designed to capture differences between careers companies by legal form. Three of the case studies were chosen to represent cases where incumbents had been converted into LEA/TEC or LEA/LEC partnerships, and two to represent cases of 'new entry' by newly established careers companies. The second criterion was designed to provide variation in the labour market environment in terms of the level of unemployment.

Table 1: Criteria for selection of case-study areas

	LEA/TEC or LEA/LEC partnership	New-entrant careers companies
Low unemployment	Bristol	Reading
High unemployment	Sheffield, Fife	Inner London

While Inner London, Sheffield and Fife all suffered high levels of unemployment, Sheffield and Fife had more developed adult guidance provision, with a wide reputation for an active approach to the field. In the case of Sheffield, this was based on the commitment of the local TEC to fund out of its reserves a dedicated adult guidance division of the careers service; in the case of Fife, the local authority supported adult guidance actively as part of an anti-poverty strategy. Both areas had a well-organised collaborative network of providers. In contrast, Bristol and Reading both enjoyed high levels of economic activity and low unemployment. Nevertheless, they too differed from each other in the extent of provision of adult guidance services. The five localities thus reveal the diversity in patterns of provision that emerged from the mid-to-the-late 1990s.

Bristol: LEA/TEC partnership; low unemployment

Bristol is a prosperous area in the South West of England with low unemployment. The local careers service is a non-profit company limited by guarantee formed as a partnership between the local authority and the local TEC. At the time of our fieldwork (1997), it combined four separate branches serving distinct functions. One of these branches provided adult guidance on a consultancy basis to companies and on a more limited scale to private clients who were charged between £45 and £170 for individual guidance services. The second branch was the mainstream careers company, which had established a city-centre guidance 'shop' serving 26,000 'customers' per year, half of them adults. The shop provided a basic information service to 80% of its customers and interviews to about 20%. The surplus from the commercial branch was used by the careers company to provide free guidance services to adults. The latter services were also subsidised by grants from the local TEC, the EU Konver programme (for redundant workers from defence-related industries) and the DfEE. The company had extensive links with employers and visits were made to over 1,000 employers each year to canvass for vacancies and advertise their services. It also had service-level agreements with local colleges to provide career counselling to college students on site, although this was limited to the statutory age groups. A third branch, funded by the TEC, provided services under the Education–Business Partnership. The fourth branch covered training activities and aimed to promote lifelong learning and career development. It delivered the TEC lifelong learning programme through various adult education projects in collaboration with employers, colleges and local community groups. This branch was funded from the TEC, under contract. In conjunction with local colleges, it ran an open-learning project, targeted at people who had been out of education for some time, and a 'Return to Learn' scheme based on the Rover and Ford EDAP. The latter subsidised employees to attend after-work courses. Other activities of the branch included an outreach service through local guidance shops, a training programme for 'key workers' in small businesses, an open-learning network and an NVQ service for employers. In all these activities, there was close collaboration with the local TEC, which had a strong commitment to the provision of guidance services to adults. By integrating training and guidance services, the careers company was able to provide a relevant and accessible service that promoted guidance to adults in an effective way.

In contrast to the limited guidance offered to adult students at the colleges, the local university had a well-resourced careers office, supported by significant inputs from large national businesses. Bristol also had a thriving private guidance sector. This was financed by charging fees to companies for redundancy and outplacement counselling. Typically, companies were charged between £500 and £5,000 per employee for these services. Recruitment agencies were also active in the local labour market, and one such agency interviewed in the project was a training provider for the TEC. Although recruits were sometimes referred to the careers service for guidance, the agency also provided guidance in-house to its clients.

Sheffield: LEA/TEC partnership; high unemployment

Sheffield is an old industrial city in the North of England with relatively high levels of unemployment. As in Bristol, the careers company is a LEA/TEC partnership. The careers company was established in April 1995 as a non-profit company limited by guarantee, with charitable status. Both the LEA and the TEC nominated seven trustees to the board of the company, to reflect stakeholder interests: schools, colleges, small and large firms, trades unions and training providers. At the time of our fieldwork (1997), adult guidance was provided on a self-funding basis through a separate specialised division. This division was funded by the TEC and by grants from the ESF and the SRB. EU funding was a significant factor and provided about 35% of the division's income.

The company operated a drop-in careers library for adults who could obtain information and, if they lived in the ESF area, a guidance interview. It was used by 50,000 people each year. The first guidance interview was free of charge, paid for by the TEC. Further guidance sessions were provided on a fee-paying basis to those earning over £300 per week, and free to those earning less than this amount and to unemployed people. Psychometric tests were offered free to the same categories of clients, and were charged at almost £100 to others. Outplacement counselling was provided as a free service to companies employing less than 50 workers, through ESF funding. Adult educational guidance was provided separately by the TEC through a Training Advice Centre. This unit employed three full-time advisers and two information officers; about 4,500 people used the service each year.

The careers company had established a network of local guidance providers and professionals who met regularly in a Network Forum to exchange experience and ideas. This was especially useful for coordinating activity with the voluntary sector and with local colleges and universities. Particular attention was paid to adults from disadvantaged groups. Outreach workers were employed to provide services to the local ethnic minorities, who formed 7% of the local population. The integration of the company into the local guidance network, and the partnership between the LEA and the TEC, had been highly successful and had resulted in an accessible and high-quality provision of guidance services for adults living in this locality. It should be noted that this collaborative approach did not spring up overnight, but had been developed for a number of years prior to the reforms of the mid-1990s. Despite its success, there was still a large unmet need for guidance. In the words of one careers company interviewee: "There is a need for core funding – why can't adult guidance be financed in the same way as young people's guidance?"

Fife: LEA/LEC partnership; high unemployment

In Fife, the partnership awarded the careers service contract (Fife Careers) was made up of the local authority, which had a long history of work on economic regeneration and social support, and Fife Enterprise (the LEC). However, in addition to Fife Careers, the local authority had supported its own Fife Adult Guidance and Education Service (FAGES). FAGES was the outcome of the integration of a number of the local authority's services, namely Adult Education, Adult Basic Education,

English for Speakers of Other Languages (ESOL) and Adult Guidance. It was based in the Community Education Department but had links to the Council's Social and Community Development Committee. At the time of our fieldwork, FAGES had the largest number of staff allocated to adult guidance in the UK, employing 14 full-time equivalents; in the UK as a whole, 55% of providers had three or fewer staff for adult guidance and a further 33% had between four and six (ICG, 1996). This reflected the authority's concern with unemployment and community regeneration. Indeed, adult guidance was identified as a top priority for the Council in its corporate objectives; it was seen as integral to its anti-poverty strategy. The economy of Fife had until recently been dominated by coal-mining, defence industries and, before that, textiles; they were all industries that had gone into major decline. At the time of our fieldwork, unemployment was 10% above the Scottish average. Inward investment had created some part-time jobs in call centres.

Fife was characterised by partnership working among a range of organisations concerned with economic regeneration. Key actors, in addition to Fife Careers, FAGES, the local authority and Fife Enterprise, included the District Office of the ES and Fife Training Information Services. This latter organisation, again based in the local authority, had its roots in the old Manpower Services Commission's Training Access Points scheme, set up in the late 1980s. The service provided independent computerised information on education and training courses throughout the UK, through training information points in libraries, jobcentres, colleges and careers services. There was also a free telephone enquiry service. Effort had been put into listing up-to-date information on local opportunities, including non-traditional, part-time and short courses, as well as open learning, in-house training, and EC co-funded initiatives run by FAGES, such as First Steps and Route One for people returning to learning or to the labour market.

FAGES coordinated the Fife Adult Guidance Network whose members all provided adult guidance, although for many it was as part of other activities such as community education, college courses, citizens' advice or placement for unemployed people. The network was supported through funding from the Scottish Office; indeed, this was the only resource that Scottish Office put into adult guidance apart from the telephone helpline. In addition, there were more informal local guidance networks in the area and local planning groups for European projects.

The main sources of income for FAGES were the local authority and the EU. Indeed, Fife was one of the most successful adult guidance providers in the UK in terms of attracting EU funding (see later in this chapter). The active networks put FAGES in an advantageous position to apply for European co-funding. There were also close links with colleges that invited FAGES in to provide independent guidance and participate in their EU co-funded projects.

While the local authority had set no performance indicators for FAGES other than targets for European funding (which have normally been exceeded), the service had set its own monitoring and evaluation systems in place. In addition, the Scottish Office had devised the Scottish Quality Management System for Education and Training (SQMS) and Fife was the first guidance service to implement this; it included nine standards of organisational activity. Targets set by the Advisory Scottish Council for Education and Training also played a role in the structuring of adult guidance in Scotland.

In some senses, the institutional framework within which adult guidance was located in Fife was more similar than in the case of our other case studies to the previous context within which careers services had worked in local authorities. Fife Careers and FAGES had a fair degree of autonomy in how they responded to needs in the area. For FAGES, there were no performance indicators or drivers working against the provision of a service for the most disadvantaged, as there were elsewhere. If clients needed a considerable amount of support to progress along various stages to the labour market, it was possible to provide this. The context of both services, within an ethos of community regeneration and anti-poverty strategies, and a well-developed network of organisations, facilitated cooperative working with a range of public-sector agencies in what was a crowded playing field. The networking meant that it was more likely that adults received independent advice, as there was a culture of referral between agents. It also facilitated maximum advantage to be taken of European funding; expertise had developed in making applications, handling the bureaucracy and managing the finances effectively in the way required by the EC, which made working with such projects cost-effective.

Inner London: new-entrant careers company; high unemployment

At the time of our fieldwork, unemployment in inner London had risen above 15%. There was a relatively large population from ethnic-minority groups, and a concentration of asylum seekers and other disadvantaged groups. The careers company was a new-entrant private company limited by shares. It was a subsidiary of a large regional conglomerate which held the contract to provide guidance services in four areas outside its home-base in Surrey. The shareholders of the parent company were a county council, some major financial institutions and some individuals. The company provided guidance services for adults, funded through contracts with the ESF, the SRB and the local authority. Target groups included unemployed people and people living in housing estates with high levels of social deprivation. However, there was no accessible high-street 'shop' where adults could easily drop in to obtain services. The main information point was housed in the same building as the local jobcentre where unemployed people registered for benefits. The adult educational guidance unit had remained under local-authority ownership and management, and struggled to retain its independence from both the careers company and the local colleges. The justification was a desire to provide unbiased and impartial advice. However, being located in the same building as the unemployment benefit office was likely to deter some potential clients, especially those seeking educational guidance. The Jobseeker's Allowance imposed a limit of 16 hours per week on attendance on a course of education or training; according to one interviewee, individuals might worry that if they were seen to be looking for a course, they would risk the loss of their income support and housing benefits. The interviewee argued that this presented a serious obstacle to the implementation of policies to promote lifelong learning.

The main source of funding for adult guidance in inner London came from the local TEC. Being a separate entity from the careers service, the TEC was not tied to purchasing guidance services from the careers service. Instead, it contracted out the guidance work to a wide range of local providers, including the careers service, but also a large number of organisations in the voluntary sector based around specific community groups, charities and colleges, as well as a network of private guidance providers. These providers of adult guidance were funded through block contracts, let on a competitive basis by the TEC; they provided a mix of free services and means-tested fee-charged services to around 3,000 clients per year. The contracts specified targets, including targets for increasing the numbers of fee-charged services provided. Although the extent of adult guidance provision funded by the TEC appeared low, the TEC also ran its own telephone helpline with a budget of £40,000 that reached out to a wider client group. In the opinion of the TEC respondent, the "problem with the [adult] guidance sector [in the borough] is that it is so fragmented".

Reflecting the low level of adult guidance provision in the boroughs, local colleges attempted to fill the gap. For example, the local Community College provided a wide range of guidance services, based on funding from a variety of sources. These included the ES (which funded a job search unit), the local borough (which funded a unit for truants), the local health authority (for mental patients), the National Association for the Care and Rehabilitation of Offenders (NACRO) (for ex-offenders) and so on. The college also had three part-time community development workers who provided services through local community groups.

Reading: new-entrant careers company; low unemployment

Reading is a prosperous 'boom town' in the South of England with low unemployment (2% in 1997) and one of the highest levels of Gross Domestic Product (GDP) per capita in the country. The local careers company is a branch of a large independent company specialising in the provision of education courses teaching English as a foreign language, and in school inspections. Unlike most other careers company organisations, it is a global company which at the time of our fieldwork had 4,000 employees world-wide and a turnover of £30 million. The company is limited by guarantee and has charitable status. It won the contract to provide careers services in 1995, and had expanded to provide the careers service for a number of other areas. This expansion was designed to protect the company against risk through the diversification of its activities. The company also claimed there were economies of scale, which allowed it to improve the quality of its services to the core client group of school pupils and school leavers. At the time of our visit, the careers service division was the fastest expanding part of the company, with a turnover of £11 million.

However, this belief in economies of scale did not extend to the provision of adult guidance services; the company had decided not to establish an adult guidance unit, as "the market is too limited to provide a worthwhile commercial prospect", according to the company's chief executive. Consequently, it had fallen to the local TEC to provide adult guidance services, which it did by contracting out services to local providers, mainly in the voluntary sector. But the various TEC initiatives in this field had been unsuccessful in generating funds from government programmes, employers or the ES. A limited residual service, including a 'Skill Bus' and a telephone helpline, had been established, funded mainly by the ESF. In addition, reserves built up from the Training for Work programme were used to finance adult guidance services through a number of voluntary-sector providers and local FE colleges. In the light of this experience, the view of the TEC was that the greatest unmet need in the conditions of a tight labour market was for adult guidance services for employees in work, to enable job-to-job transitions that could underpin flexibility in the labour market. "If the objective of a learning society is to develop skills, you don't do it by focusing resources on marginal groups such as the unemployed" (TEC respondent).

In these circumstances, the main activities in the field of adult guidance in Reading were carried out by small voluntary groups catering for severely disadvantaged groups in the labour market. One such group, based at the local FE college, provided services to the long-term unemployed, women returnees to work, disabled adults, ethnic minorities and ex-offenders. However, such services were small-scale and faced budget cuts. The only disadvantaged group with a relatively secure level of provision was ex-offenders, who benefited from an innovative project based at the local probation service. In contrast, the local university had a large careers office and was well resourced, with strong financial and in-kind backing from employers, who stood to benefit from a well-informed pool of graduate labour.

Comparisons

Overall, the five localities included in the case studies displayed noticeable differences in the structure of provision of adult guidance services. Broadly, adult guidance services appeared to be better developed in Bristol, Sheffield and Fife than in Inner London and Reading. These differences appeared to be connected more with the organisational form of guidance provider organisations than with the state of the local labour markets; that is, the differences reflected different provider orientations rather than the needs of the local population.

While both Sheffield and Inner London suffered high levels of unemployment, Sheffield had more developed adult guidance provision, based on a commitment of the local TEC to fund services out of its reserves, the existence of a dedicated adult guidance division of the careers service, and a well-organised collaborative network of providers. Similarly, Fife, another area of high unemployment, benefited from the commitment of the local authority to economic regeneration and combating poverty, manifested in resources being made available for adult guidance, closely linked to educational services for the disadvantaged. In Inner London, although the local TEC had a commitment to adult guidance, it did not work in close collaboration with the careers company, and provision was fragmented among a plethora of voluntary and community groups. Local colleges worked hard to plug the gaps but their primary focus was on attracting students on to courses rather than on the provision of independent advice. Moreover, they struggled to attract funding from a diverse set of funding bodies.

In contrast, the remaining two localities, Bristol and Reading, both enjoyed high levels of economic activity and low unemployment. Nevertheless, they too differed in the extent of provision of adult guidance services. In Bristol, the local careers service had a dedicated section providing adult guidance on a consultancy basis to companies and also, to a more limited extent, to individuals. A city-centre guidance shop provided highly visible services to the public, with a large proportion of adults among the users of this service. There was close collaboration with the local TEC, which had a strong commitment to the provision of guidance services to adults. In addition, there was a thriving private sector, which attracted a substantial amount of business from employers. By contrast, in Reading, which had similarly low unemployment, the provision of adult guidance was extremely limited. The careers company had withdrawn from the provision of adult guidance and viewed it as an unprofitable market. And the local TEC, although recognising the importance of adult guidance, both for employees and for the marginalised unemployed, struggled to obtain funding and appeared less willing to use its own reserves to finance adult guidance services than was the case in the Bristol area.

A key factor in determining the extent of provision, therefore, appeared to be the way in which the careers services and the TECs/LEC interacted in different cases. Where interaction was close and collaborative, the transition to a contracted-out careers service appeared to have generated a dynamic and innovative approach to the expansion of guidance services for adults. This interaction seemed to be best achieved in cases where there was a formal organisational partnership on which to base the work of the careers service. More specifically, it appeared to be beneficial for the careers services and the TECs/LEC to be fused together in a formal organisational structure based on the formation of careers companies as LEA/TEC or LEA/LEC partnerships. Elsewhere, in cases where such interaction was absent or made more difficult by the entry of independent careers companies without close links to local TEC structures, the provision of adult guidance was placed on a less coherent and more fragmented basis. In these cases, the TEC appeared to have less interest and ability to stimulate the provision of adult guidance services, and the careers services were more focused on the provision of commercially viable services to the statutory groups in schools and colleges. Moreover, TEC-funded contracted-out provision here was fragmented and small-scale, and failed to benefit from the economies of scale which the large independent careers companies identified as important in their statutory activity.

Funding

Funding for adult guidance has depended significantly on the ability of careers companies to generate surpluses, and on the policy of the local TEC/LEC towards funding provision through careers services or networks of independent providers. It has also depended on the ability of these organisations to access external contract funding from a wide variety of sources, prominent among which are the ESF, the regional SRB, and to a lesser extent other government departments such as the Home Office (in the case of ex-offenders) and charities. There has been substantial funding for educational guidance in colleges, funded through the FEFCs, and for career guidance for undergraduates, arguably an already privileged group, through university careers offices. Apart from this, adult guidance services have depended on the ability of individuals to pay individual fees for services, but to date the take-up of such services has appeared to be low. It is argued that there is only a limited market for adult guidance services, although – as noted in Chapter Four – there is a thriving private sector for redundancy counselling and outplacement services. This private-sector activity is funded substantially by employers; on the whole, apart from ex-military personnel, it is only employees of the larger corporate employers who benefit.

Although in the mid-1990s 86% of careers services provided guidance to adults (ICG, 1996), variations were reported in the sources of funding across the different parts of the UK. Local-authority funding was more significant in Scotland (where 41% of companies reported it as their main source of income for providing services to adults) than in England (26%). ESF was identified as providing the main source of income for 29% of Scottish careers companies, compared with only 9% in England. TECs were the principal funder for 36% of companies in England, whereas in Scotland LECs were the principal funder for adult guidance in only 29% of careers companies. Only 15% of English careers companies relied on only one source of funding, compared with 46% of Scottish companies. Moreover, clients were likely to be asked to pay for some services in England, but not in general in Scotland where fee paying tended to be regarded by guidance professionals as unacceptable to the client group. In Scotland, provision has been more closely integrated into regional economic and social planning strategies (Rees and Bartlett, 1999b).

Fife has been arguably one of the most successful areas in Britain in attracting EC co-funding to support its adult guidance activities and in making strategic use of it to address local needs. In Chapter Three, we examined the role of the EC in supporting adult guidance. Here, we explore the conditions in Fife that resulted in such a significant EC investment in adult guidance. It was not the careers company, Fife Careers, that was the prime mover in securing EC co-funding, but FAGES, based in the local authority's Community Education Department. Fife Council regarded it as crucial to integrate guidance and adult education to ensure that the learning provision was related to local needs and opportunities were provided for progression. Adult guidance services in Fife were seen as an integral part of the local authority's anti-poverty and community-regeneration policies.

FAGES had a strong relationship with Fife Careers; both sets of staff had roots in the LEA. Fife was one of the few LEAs that paid guidance workers on the teachers' salary scale, and Fife Careers was the only predominantly graduate careers company in Scotland. There was a particularly strong network of regional and local partners involved with the anti-poverty policies in Fife, and they were mobilised for bids to the EC. Projects targeted in particular the long-term unemployed, women returnees and other disadvantaged groups.

The main sources of income for FAGES were the EU and the local authority. Eastern Scotland had been designated as an area eligible for funding under Objective 2 (regions in decline) and Objective 3 (combating long-term unemployment and integration of young people). It also had recognised status as a former coal-mining area (which made it eligible for RECHAR) and as a community affected by the decline in the fishing industry (for which PESCA was available). The active networks put FAGES in an advantageous position to apply for European co-funding for projects under these programmes. The focus on disadvantaged groups meant that FAGES was also eligible for many strands in the EU's EMPLOYMENT Community initiative, such as ADAPT (for workers in declining industries) and INTEGRA (for the most disadvantaged in the labour market). The adult education and guidance budgets were used as matched funding for EC projects. In 1997, European funding supported 45% of FAGES staff costs.

In the same year, seven applications were made by FAGES, for a total of nearly £200,000 of EU money, to provide 50,000 hours of guidance and pre-vocational training for unemployed people and those at risk of unemployment. Considerable expertise had been developed in making applications, handling the bureaucratic procedures and managing the finances effectively in the way required by the EC, thus making working with such projects cost-effective for the applicants. There were also close links with colleges, which invited FAGES in to provide independent guidance and participate in their EU co-funded projects. In addition, as part of Fife Council, FAGES had taken advantage of EU programmes focusing on disadvantaged regions and individuals to co-fund adult guidance services as part of the local authority's social and economic regeneration policy. As a spokesperson for the Economic Development Department at Fife Council observed:

> "Adult guidance is a top priority in the Council in terms of corporate objectives. It is part of the anti-poverty strategy. Training is seen as a way out of poverty so there is a huge emphasis on it, despite the budget. There is support from the county councillors. The Leader of the Administration is convinced that guidance and training and placement are the way out of poverty."

Overall, Fife had a well-developed infrastructure and active network which facilitated the integration of adult guidance into social and economic regeneration activities. A person was employed full-time to prepare bids for European funding for the partnerships between the local colleges and the Council. There was a move towards developing a Fife Training Strategy and efforts were made to ensure that applications for funding fitted in with that strategy. Problems of competition between providers and compromising of impartiality, to which infrastructure arrangements can give rise, appeared to be less prevalent in Fife than elsewhere. Its local-authority base, its close working networks, and its focus on economic regeneration and anti-poverty strategies were important elements in shaping the priority given to and use made by FAGES of EC co-funding for adult guidance.

Access to adult guidance

This research has shown some evidence that there was a substantially different outcome with regard to the provision of adult guidance services depending on the types of companies winning contracts following the marketisation of careers services. The main finding is that LEA/TEC and LEA/LEC partnerships were more concerned to provide adult guidance than were the new entrants, which concentrated on the provision of core services to the statutory client groups. The latter did so not only for commercial reasons, but also because of a lack of integration of services with the TECs. Does this mean that the entry of new providers or the expansion of the 'independents' should have been discouraged? We do not think that this is a necessary implication. The new entrants claimed to have been able to provide a cost-effective service, and, by expanding, to have gained economies of scale. If further contracting competitions had been carried out, it is possible that the more dynamic companies would have expanded into new areas and that ultimately guidance services in England would have been delivered by a handful of the more aggressive and cost-effective providers. This could have been a beneficial outcome in some respects, although it is unclear whether its long-term effect on the provision of adult guidance services would have been beneficial or damaging.

Across the UK, the provision of adult guidance remains patchy, as it was at the time of our fieldwork. The quality and range of services offered to users depends very much on the accident of where one happens to live. Moreover, this spatial variation bears no relationship to need as expressed by differences in labour-market conditions. Where adult guidance services are provided on a free or means-tested basis, they are generally only provided to users living within the area covered by the service provider in question. A possible solution to the problem of spatial differentiation would be to introduce a means of funding 'cross-border' flows of users. This could be done through a national funding formula, perhaps based on a system of vouchers, similar to that used by the Corporation of London in financing 'out of area' provision of training and education for its adult learners. The new Learndirect website and Learning and Work databank with telephone helpline will need to be backed up by substantial funding for referrals to avoid making more visible the existing inequalities in the pattern of guidance provision.

The general fragmentation and patchiness of provision for adults are intensified in the access to services by disadvantaged groups. Although many careers services and TECs/LECs have been sensitive to the needs of disadvantaged groups such as the long-term unemployed, women returnees to work, ex-offenders and ethnic-minority groups, there has been a lack of strategic focus towards them. Guidance services for such groups have often relied on the activity of voluntary and community groups operating on a relatively small scale. Colleges of further education have been particularly active in this field, although often with a primary interest in attracting users to the courses on offer. Moreover, employer biases against certain categories of workers – for example, older workers – have remained a structural problem which guidance services have been ill equipped to tackle.

Equity

A survey of English careers service companies on gender equality found that only a third had a sound equal-opportunities policy that included an agenda for policy and practice and a structure for implementation (Rolfe, 1999). Paradoxically, those with policies in place did not necessarily have good practice, while good practices were identified among some companies that did not appear to have an equal-opportunities policy. Company policy documents did not particularly reflect issues in the local labour market. They also tended to be generic, grouping the equality dimensions together. This can be problematic, as some dimensions require different policies to be effective. Gender-disaggregated statistics, for example, have proved to be a very useful tool for organisations seeking to monitor the effectiveness of their gender-equality policies. However, racial monitoring is politically problematic even though it can be effective, disability monitoring is fraught with conceptual difficulties, and Stonewall, the gay and lesbian lobby group that has just drafted a code of practice for employers on good employment practices, advises against monitoring for sexual orientation.

The survey showed that responsibility for equal opportunities was not defined in some services. No staff were allocated to have special responsibility for the topic. Moreover, most had no policies in place to deal with instances of discrimination encountered, nor did they have action plans to address gender inequality. Effective partnerships were an important key to success in gender-equality work; hence careers companies with good relations with TECs were well positioned (Rolfe, 1999).

The study confirmed that target-setting by DfEE and government offices, and meeting the obligations set out in the Requirements and

Guidance for careers services, set their agenda. The Requirements and Guidance document had two references to gender equality, one on challenging stereotyped attitudes of employment and training providers, the other on working with primary schools to combat sex stereotyping. Some respondents felt that meeting targets had "consumed time which was previously spent in development work, including gender equality" (Rolfe, 1999, p 90). As one respondent said:

> "Although it's probably changing this year, in previous years we have been so tightly tied by targets that we haven't had time to do any of the development-type things. We have had to have staff heads down, banging out the interviews and action plans in order to meet targets. So we've probably lost some of the work we've done in the past. If you were to go back 10 years, you might find there were a lot more interesting things going on with regard to gender."

However, Rolfe detected that there was a feeling among careers services that gender might be shifting up the agenda, because it had been identified as of concern to the Labour government. Commitment from the top and identified resources for equality work were identified as crucial to success. The changes mooted in contractual arrangements should also be beneficial to gender equality and other developmental work. Rolfe found that the English careers companies did not tend to have many examples of positive action measures in place, confirming our impression that it is in the third sector that most of these examples are to be found.

Conclusions

In the preceding chapters, we have argued that career guidance services for adults have an increasing role to play in a labour market which is becoming increasingly turbulent, and in which interrupted spells of employment, unemployment, retraining and re-skilling are becoming a more common pattern of career for many individuals. Both educational and vocational guidance need to be given more prominence if they are to support the participation of individuals in the more complex, knowledge-based 'learning society' which such changes involve. Alongside these labour-market changes, the organisation and structure of the career guidance system has been changing too, in quite radical ways. As yet, however, these changes have not resulted in a comprehensive expansion of lifelong guidance services that could meet the needs of individuals facing rapid and unexpected changes in their career path through adult life. Government strategy has remained geared mainly to the skills growth model of the learning society, in which public provision of guidance services are justified in relation to narrow economic criteria. Personal career development has remained the responsibility of the individual, and social integration considerations have only recently begun to be addressed, since the advent of the Labour government. The provision of adult guidance services remains patchy and inadequately resourced even in terms of the conventional approach. There are severe problems of funding which is increasingly managed through private fees, and problems of access for disadvantaged groups have still not been adequately addressed. In contrast, the core labour market is better served by a number of large employers who engage outplacement agencies, and in the provision of guidance for graduates from at least some institutions of higher education. If an informed choice of the new learning and career opportunities of the future is to become a lifelong concern of the majority of the labour force, much more attention will need to be given to the provision of a comprehensive adult guidance system for the learning society.

SIX

France

Introduction

France has a well-developed, pluralistic adult guidance system based around a number of different client groups. A number of separate and distinct organisations exist to provide guidance services to individuals at different stages of their career and at different points of transition between training and work. Young adults are assisted by a centralised state-organised careers service as in many other European countries, including the UK. But beyond that, a variety of other organisations and initiatives exists to assist individuals through their various stages of lifelong learning and career development. Young adults who experience social difficulties can turn for assistance to a system of 'local missions' (*Missions Locales*) for both vocational and social guidance. The main French adult training organisation (AFPA) provides an integrated guidance service to support national and local training and re-training programmes. Employees who are considering a career change are entitled to a leave of absence from work to undertake a skills assessment with a guidance component. One of the main providers of skills assessments works closely with women labour-market returnees. Employed executives have recourse to their own organisation for career development and guidance. Finally, unemployed people can access guidance services through the extensive network of guidance counsellors employed by the National Employment Agency (ANPE). Thus, in France, there is a complex mosaic of organisations which offer custom-made guidance services to different segments of the labour market and to individuals at different stages in their lifetime career.

Many of the organisations that provide guidance services are in the 'social economy' (Danvers and Monsanson, 1997). Social enterprises have been established under a 1901 Law as *Associations*, roughly equivalent to 'not-for-profit' organisations in the UK and USA, but with a more participative management structure. This 'third sector' has traditionally played a more important role in French society and the French economy than in most other European countries. The role of third-sector organisations in the area of social welfare services has also grown dramatically since the 1983 Decentralisation Act, which extended the role of local authorities and municipalities in the provision of welfare services; many have been keen to involve the organisations already working in the social economy (Mizrahi-Tchernonog, 1991).

Examples of relevant social enterprises discussed in this chapter include:

- the *Missions Locales* – local multi-functional organisations that aim to provide guidance services together with other forms of social advice to young people in difficulty;
- AFPA (*Association pour la Formation Professionelle des Adultes*), which provides adult vocational guidance targeted towards unemployed people and disabled people;
- the *Retravailler* (Back to Work) group of organisations, which specialises in providing training and guidance to women labour-market returnees.

These kinds of organisations form the core of the adult guidance system in France.

This chapter charts the key features of these various organisations, starting with those dealing with young adults, demonstrating the special French concern with the 'social insertion' of young people and the plethora of services targeted at groups that are disadvantaged in the labour market. It goes on to show the way in which lifelong training and guidance services for adults have been integrated into a common organisational structure in France. This is followed by a description of a particular feature of the system in France, the 'skills assessment', to which employees are regularly entitled. It develops the theme that the delivery of skills assessment takes place in a quasi-market funded by employers rather then directly by the state. It then considers the types of providers of guidance services for a wide range of social groups. The chapter concludes with descriptions of the distinct services provided for executives and for unemployed people.

Guidance for school leavers

The guidance system for young people in initial vocational education is highly centralised and professionalised, and provided by a state-administered careers service (*Centres d'Information et Orientation* – CIOs). At the time of our fieldwork in 1996 the Ministry of Education employed

3,700 guidance counsellors in 518 CIOs throughout France. They work mainly in secondary schools and universities, but the CIOs are also open to the general public, who can access careers information and see a counsellor free of charge. Backing all this up on the information side is the National Office for Information on Education and Occupations (Office National d'Information sur les Enseignenments et les Professions – ONISEP), a centralised information office that provides documentation to CIO guidance counsellors. ONISEP was created in 1970 when it was considered that information was the key element in career guidance.

The Ministry of Education is heavily involved with Euronetwork, a European database on career guidance, visual conferencing and the Internet. It also participates in EC action programmes such as LEONARDO DA VINCI in order to assist youth mobility in Europe through the provision of information and contacts. Five CIOs hold a special responsibility for European issues and provide specialised information about jobs abroad. They operate as resource centres for other CIOs on a regional basis. Links have been established with guidance services in other European countries, such as the UK European guidance centre based in Bradford, that act as a repository of information about guidance and mobility (the European network of information centres mentioned in Chapter Three).

The CIOs have established a well-organised system for tracking school leavers. Guidance counsellors prepare a skills assessment of pupils when they leave school. This can lead on to a plan for further guidance or training, and this information is kept by the school to assist the follow-up process. As part of their educational mission, schools are supposed to know the destination of every school leaver. School leavers are therefore followed up closely for the first year after leaving school. These activities are funded jointly by the Ministry of Education and the regions.

Guidance for young adults at risk of social exclusion

The *Missions Locales* (MLs) are inter-institutional organisations formed in 1982 as *Associations* under the 1901 Law. They were set up as a result of the influential Schwartz Report, instigated by the late President Mitterand, on the professional 'insertion' of young people between the ages of 16 and 25. The concept of social 'insertion' is the positive counterpart of the more widely-known negative concept of social 'exclusion' and was much debated in France in the 1980s during a period of high youth unemployment. MLs deal with housing, health, finance and training, as well as jobs. They are intended to adopt an holistic approach, and to provide all their services under the same roof, and on a local basis. They are therefore organised on three basic principles: inter-institutionality, an holistic approach, and local delivery. The decision to create a ML is made by the local mayor, who becomes the president of a board that includes social partners, school representatives, and representatives of the local CIO. Indeed, all the relevant public services are represented on the board of an ML, including representatives from the Ministries of Social Affairs, Education, Youth and Sport and so on. Members of staff who work in a ML include people on secondment from the CIO and ANPE (see below), as well as social workers and teachers for continuing education.

The MLs provide an integrated service to help disadvantaged youth obtain access to housing, training, healthcare and income support in order to assist their 'social insertion'. By 1994, 250 MLs had been established throughout France, together with a further 420 smaller branches known as PAIOs (*Permanence d'Acceuil d'Information et d'Orientation* – Offices for Advice, Information and Guidance). In 1995 the MLs and PAIOs together had 5,000 employees, and offered services to over 950,000 young people between the ages of 16 and 25. It should be noted that although ML counsellors usually have a university-level education, they do not need to have a professional qualification in psychology. Although they are criticised for this by some of the other guidance organisations, it was argued by the managers we interviewed that this gives the director the flexibility needed to select a team able to meet the varied needs of the client group.

MLs are financed from three sources – the state, the region and the town, in equal proportions – whereas the PAIOs only receive state funds. The amount of funding received depends on the number of young people in the area, how many clients were dealt with in the previous year and the number of unemployed youths (in other words, funding is capitation-based). Their purpose is to work with disadvantaged young people described as being 'in difficulty' (*les jeunes en difficulté*) and to help them integrate into society. Working at a local level, they help young people to find housing, training and employment. Guidance is provided to their clients as part of this process, and is intended to overcome social exclusion. This is recognised to be caused by a complex set of factors, not simply restricted to unemployment or to low levels of education and training. The guidance services provided are supplemented by a process of 'social guidance' to redress such social disadvantage.

While MLs provide both a vocational and a social guidance service for young people in difficulties, the main requests for help are for jobs and training – to get on to a paid training course a young person is obliged to pass through an ML. When the first interview is held, an evaluation of his or her social situation is made, including social status, family circumstances, personality and level of education. All clients then receive a follow-up interview with a counsellor who decides whether the priority is for vocational or social guidance. Vocational guidance includes an evaluation of basic knowledge, evaluation of level of French (for example, in the case of immigrants), and level of motivation. Clients are always followed up, for up to three years after their consultation; the follow-up procedures include keeping in touch with firms that employ youths, in order to track their progress.

'Social' guidance covers wider problems that young people face, including housing, welfare benefits and so on. The aim is to give young people a clear path to employment and to support them in achieving their integration into training and employment. The activities of social guidance include a leisure and sports programme, and a theatre programme that has had a surprising success, leading to plans to use theatrical techniques in work with withdrawn youngsters. In Paris, there is a specialist CIO addressing the needs of youths in trouble with the law and MLs work closely with it – for example, in training their personnel.

In 1995, the Paris ML had 1,300 clients. Overall, it estimated that it achieved a 70% placement rate. Although it is designed to cater for 16 to 25 year olds, in practice the average age of ML clients is about 21 to 25 years. There are no state benefits for under-25 year olds in the form of income support; local allowances are available but they have no minimum threshold. Once over 25, an individual is eligible for a state income benefit, but not before. Young unemployed people can only get an allowance if they go on a paid training scheme. In Paris, free healthcare and housing are also available, and there is a local allowance for those who can prove they are active job seekers. Hence, unsurprisingly, a major group among ML clients comprises young people who have lost their jobs but are not eligible for benefits. Although most clients attend by their own free choice, MLs have also to deal with disaffected and unmotivated youths sent to them by social services.

Guidance through skills assessment

A unique element of the French guidance system is the provision for all employees to take a leave of absence from work, once every five years, for a period of training and 'skills assessment' (*bilan de compétences*). The Ministry of Labour introduced this right under a Law enacted in 1991. The skills assessment is now a main locale for the provision of adult career guidance. It provides an audit of personal and professional skills acquired through education and training. Firms are enthusiastic about the concept, as they recognise a need to evaluate the skills of their employees. The Law allows employees who have been employed for more than five years to take up to 24 hours' paid leave for skills assessments over a two-month period.

The origin of these arrangements dates back to 1978 when the law on continuing education at work was modified to give employees a right to a leave of absence to undertake a training course, funded by a compulsory levy on employers with firms over a certain size. Employers pay 1-1.5% of their wages bill into a training fund known as FONGECIF (*Fond Gestion Congé Individuel Formation*). Contributions are also made by the state at local, regional and national levels, and further funding is derived from EC programmes. The fund is the main source of finance for adult training in France, in addition to whatever training firms carry out themselves directly. The arrangement is similar to the old Industrial Training Boards in the UK, of which only the Construction Industry Training Board survives. Since 1991, between 15% and 20% of the fund has been allocated to the skills-assessment programme.

The fund holds a list of preferred providers of skills-assessments. Individuals who take advantage of the programme are free to choose a provider from the list for their assessment. Provider organisations therefore compete with one another for clients. The fact that there is competition between independent providers to provide skills-assessment services that are provided free at the point of delivery indicates a quasi-market form of public-service delivery. Quality is assured by registration on the list of preferred providers. In practice, the funds for the different sectors have different criteria. In the engineering sector, for example, assessors must have a psychologist in their team.

The quasi-market in skills assessment is highly competitive, and new training, recruiting and consulting organisations have entered the market. The providers include a variety of non-profit organisations, each of which focuses on a specific segment of the quasi-market for adult guidance. Consequently, an important characteristic of the system is the way in which it tries to 'catch' disadvantaged groups by provision of specialised guidance services for young adults, trainees, women returnees and unemployed people, as well as employees looking for a career change.

Three trends can be observed in the evolution of the practice of skills assessment from different providers:

- the emergence of self-development portfolios;
- the design of career projects including an element of career counselling;
- the development of techniques of computer-assisted career guidance.

Skills assessment is designed to produce a personal statement which is developed in consultation with a trained guidance counsellor. An important aspect is that the assessment, written up by assessor and assessed, is legally a private document for use by the client. It is designed to assist an individual's self-development, along the lines of the personal development model of the learning society outlined in the introduction. Sometimes employers want to see it, which can give rise to a conflict of interest. Another difficulty is that the system was initially designed for people with low levels of knowledge and skill. As a result, having a skills assessment began to have a stigma attached to it. Also, individuals were concerned that applying for an assessment might be seen by their employer as implying a lack of long-term commitment. Some firms discouraged workers from seeking an assessment. Accordingly, take-up of the scheme has been lower than originally expected.

Nevertheless, in 1994, 50,000 skills assessments were carried out, and the figure rose to 60,000 in 1995. Until now, the system seems to have provided a high-quality service, but there are a multiplicity of organisations and programmes, and it remains to be seen how it will develop in the future. It is more comprehensive in its coverage of different social groups than the systems found in the other countries studied in this book. The drawback is the way in which the fragmented nature of provision generates inequality in levels of service between the various client groups, depending on the efficiency of the provider organisations involved.

Providers of skills assessments

The main organisations which have entered the quasi-market for skills assessment as providers of adult guidance include AFPA, the Inter-

Institutional Skills Assessment Centres (*Centres Interinstitutionels de Bilans de Compétences* – CIBC) and *Retravailler*.

Association pour la Formation Professionnelle des Adultes

The Adult Vocational Training Association (AFPA) is an *Association* working in the field of guidance. Its origins lie in the programmes to re-train the workforce as part of national planning for post-war reconstruction in the 1950s, but it was established in its present form as a tripartite organisation involved in the provision of training and guidance services in 1966. The Minister of Labour nominates the president of the board of AFPA, whose members consist of representatives of the state, the unions and the employers. AFPA has two main missions. The first, and most important, is professional (vocational) training for both employed and unemployed people. The second is adult career guidance. This latter mission has developed more rapidly since the 1980s with the increase in unemployment. It provides career guidance alongside, and integrated with, its training function. It also has a department dedicated to independent skills assessment work.

AFPA is a large organisation which in 1996 employed 6,000 trainers and 500 occupational psychologists who guided adults and helped them to assess their occupational skills and their potential. It provided training to some 150,000 clients, either in its own centres or within firms. AFPA emphasises the importance of integrating career guidance into the training programme. Each region has developed an 'Employment Space' department open to individuals alongside the regular training sessions. Job search techniques are included in the training, and clients are able to use the 'Employment Space' to look for jobs. Training and guidance programmes are also delivered directly to companies. To give just one example, AFPA has organised a nationwide project for France Telecom which involved the employment of 50 work psychologists for a period of eight months to provide skills assessments for 1,300 members of the company's workforce.

Until the early 1980s, clients came mainly through referrals from the unemployment benefit offices. Since then, AFPA has been increasingly open to direct approaches from clients, and has recently established open 'shops' for the public. In addition, clients may come to AFPA on the basis of a leave of absence from their employer; by law, having worked for a minimum of a two-year period, employees are entitled to up to one year's absence to attend a training course. AFPA has been involved in skills assessment since the programme was introduced and has created its own assessment centre to carry out skills assessment and guidance work. AFPA guidance counsellors also specialise in entry guidance, to help people choose an appropriate form of training to fit their needs.

Before 1994, AFPA had received a global budget from the state covering 90% of its expenditure. However, the contract (*contrat de progrès*) for the period 1994–98 heralded a significant change in funding arrangements and hence a transition in working practices. The core contract was based on a capitation formula: a cost-per-case contract, rising to a ceiling. It stipulated the number of hours' training, the number of clients, and the cost-per-hour up to a set limit. At the time of our fieldwork, the amount of self-finance required had increased from 10% to 30%. Part of the self-financed work is carried out for local firms and part through contracts with local authorities. AFPA has, therefore, increasingly entered into competition for work with other large training organisations in the private sector in both its training and guidance activities. It was already possible to detect a change in the business ethic of the organisation, and a change in the language of management; AFPA's daily discourse now included references to clients rather than trainees. When negotiating with firms, staff found it useful to be able to present AFPA as a public-service body, thereby meeting less resistance from unions than private-sector organisations might encounter. AFPA managers who we interviewed considered that the new contract system had been a success, as it offered them greater autonomy and more flexibility to respond to local needs. It had encouraged a new more proactive approach to marketing and to approaching firms to negotiate new business. AFPA had accordingly developed a commercial marketing strategy and a clear aim to expand its level of activity.

Overall, AFPA claims to achieve a 60–70% job-placement rate. If the placement rate falls below 50% on any course, then that course may be closed down. In some fields, such as electronics, it is not unusual for AFPA to achieve a 100% job-placement rate. AFPA also provides training for setting up small firms, although this is a minor part of its activity; in the Ile de France in 1995, for example, the organisation trained just 240 people in business start-up.

Centres Interinstitutionels de Bilans de Compétences

The Ministry of Labour established the first CIBCs in 1985 on an experimental basis, as an initiative by the then Minister of Labour, Michel

Delebarre, to provide new services for both young people and adults. Following the success of the pilot scheme, the Ministry's *Délégation à la Formation Professionnelle* gave funds to the regions (*départements*) to create a national network of CIBCs, of which 26 were established in 1991. The CIBCs were set up either as *Associations* under the 1901 Law, or as Public Interest Organisations (*Groupements d'Interest Publique* – GIPs). In either case, they are partnership organisations that bring together a variety of institutions operating in the field of career guidance, including guidance counsellors from the Ministry of Education, and psychologists from the national training agency (AFPA). It was intended that CIBCs would be resource centres for the partners, as well as providers in their own right of career guidance in the form of skills assessments.

As part of our fieldwork, interviews were held with the Paris CIBC, a GIP set up as an agency of the Ministry of Education. Initially its board was composed of representatives drawn from *Retravailler*, AFPA, and the National Employment Agency (*Agence Nationale pour l'Emploi*, ANPE). At the time of the interview in May 1996 the competition for clients was becoming ferocious given that the income of providers depended on the number of clients served. Despite having representation on the board of the CIBC, the *Retravailler* organisation had subsequently ceased to be involved and had set up its own provider unit to compete with the CIBC. This had created problems, since the CIBC was also meant to be a resource centre for *Retravailler* and the other partner organisations. Nevertheless, Paris CIBC was carrying out about 400 assessments each year. It had five full-time equivalent counsellors and a documentalist.

Many of the clients of the CIBC were individuals taking leave of absence from work for a skills assessment. Over time, the mix of clients had shifted from being mainly unemployed people to include also a large proportion of people in paid employment, who benefited from the right to leave of absence for skills assessment paid for through the central fund. Increasingly, clients were required by their employer to attend, rather than coming voluntarily. Often a firm would refer employees with specific difficulties with regard to the firm's human resource development programme. Paris CIBC would have liked to work more closely with firms in setting strategies for guidance, and in promoting a more developmental approach.

Another main group of clients comprised unemployed people referred and funded by the unemployment office. This had been a main route to the CIBC before the 1991 Law on skills assessment was passed. Clients referred to the Paris CIBC from the unemployment office appeared to receive lower priority in receipt of the service. They faced a three-month waiting list and were allocated a different-sized time slot. Those coming from the unemployment pool were given 18 hours at most, while those coming with a leave of absence from employers were allowed a maximum of 24 hours (there was a minimum standard of nine hours' service; if the provider offered less than this, they were not paid; equally, they were not paid for more than 18 or 24 hours of service, respectively). The manager of the Paris CIBC thought that the unemployment office sent only those people for a skills assessment who they thought would be most likely to get a job, with the effect that those who most needed the service were not getting it.

Retravailler

Typical of the guidance providers in the French social economy is the *Retravailler* organisation, set up by sociologist Evelyne Sullerot in 1974 under the 1901 Law on *Associations*. *Retravailler* now has 14 centres throughout France and has established a European network with an especially strong link with an equivalent Italian organisation (see Chapter Eight). It was established with the aim of providing guidance services to women labour-market returnees (Périer, 1990). Its client group gradually expanded and today about 30% of its clients are men. Guidance services are provided to adults over the age of 25 years; the average age of clients is 30 to 35 years, with a range of 20 to 55 years. *Retravailler* depends on contract funding from the state for 95% of its income. This includes funding from the French Ministry for Women and from a variety of government programmes, as well as from competitive tendering for funds from regional training budgets, supplemented by funds from the ESF. Services for registered unemployed people are paid for by the unemployment benefit office. Guidance services are also provided to individuals on the basis of a means-tested fee; this accounts for the remaining 5% of the income. However, the funding base is not secure, and in comparison with the more formal institutions (ANPE and the *MLs*), it is a niche service provider, highly dependent on contract funding in a competitive quasi-market.

    Retravailler is a registered provider of skills assessments. The market for such assessments has become more competitive as private outplacement companies have moved into the provision of guidance and skills assessment services. However, in the view of *Retravailler*, these organisations tend to have strong links to employers and are not providing neutral guidance.

The funding base of the Paris *Retravailler* has been diminishing. In 1987, it had 600 trainees; at the time of our fieldwork it had only 250. The interviewees felt that there was less provision for women returnees than there used to be, as state funding had been reduced. Moreover, funding bodies were looking more and more for short-term results in terms of job placements achieved, rather than the personal-development outcomes which guidance counsellors were trying to promote.

Retravailler carries out work in skills assessment, and training in how to adjust to change; teaching is offered in transferable skills and communication skills; and pre-training orientation concerning the labour market in provided. It also carries out so-called 'deep counselling' sessions (*sessions d'orientations aprofondit*) for ANPE (see later). Although university entrance requirements are often too high to accommodate women returnees, there is a law that gives women with three children the right to take a test to enter a training course to become a teacher. *Retravailler* tries to raise clients to the level where they can succeed in these tests.

Guidance services for executives

The Association for the Employment of Executives (*Association pour l'Emplois des Cadres* – APEC) provides guidance services to managerial employees with a university education working in private companies, known as *cadres*. Its counterpart in the UK would be the now defunct Professional and Executive Register. It is an *Association* established in 1966 (under the 1901 Law) as a partnership venture between employees' and employers' organisations. It has an income of 360 million francs a year, funded by a 0.6% levy on the wages bill. At the time of our fieldwork, APEC employed 500 people, half of whom worked in the Paris area, and had branches in 16 towns throughout France. APEC offers its services to its client group free of charge. In addition to providing guidance services to both university graduates and to redundant and unemployed executives, it also provides recruitment services to employers. Its strength lies in bringing together both sides of the executive labour market, including guidance and recruitment, under one roof.

The main objective of APEC is to provide accurate up-to-date information on labour supply and demand for its section of the labour market. To this end it disseminates information about job vacancies and helps firms to draw up job descriptions. It also undertakes surveys of the labour market and training sector. It has a partnership relationship with the university careers service. APEC is seeking to promote a new image of its users, not as job seekers but as providers of useful skills to firms. It operates on the basis that *cadres* are sufficiently well educated to be able to analyse and process the information provided. The main techniques include: preparing and disseminating documents; supporting self-study; servicing reflection groups; providing individual professional guidance; supplying information about the labour market and skill requirements; and offering training opportunities in small-business start-up.

Guidance for unemployed people

The final major provider of adult career guidance in France that we describe here is the *Agence Nationale pour l'Emploi* (National Employment Agency–ANPE). This is the state organisation responsible for dealing with and registering unemployed people. At the time of our fieldwork, ANPE had 16,000 employees who provided services to three million unemployed people. Its 1,000 guidance counsellors were closely involved in the initial interview process. ANPE's mission is to give all clients who register access to career guidance. All clients should leave ANPE with a career goal, and an action plan or a job. Beyond this initial guidance service, further guidance work is contracted out to other professional guidance organisations. Providers compete for contracts with ANPE to supply these services. ANPE counsellors are involved in the assessment of the competitors and in quality evaluation of their services. Up to 800 organisations enter the competition, and up to 200 organisations are selected and put on a register of preferred providers (which includes inter alia the *Retravailler* organisation). This competitive system represents a further quasi-market for adult guidance provision in the French model.

The job of the guidance counsellors is to interview unemployed people, to look for job opportunities among firms, to contact recruitment officers, and to refer more difficult cases (*les publics en difficultés*) on for further guidance. Skills assessments can be prescribed for an individual or for specific groups, and counsellors may ask the local CIBC or another provider organisation to carry out this work. Despite having access to a large budget for this work, our interviewees reported that difficulties were sometimes encountered in spending it, because many unemployed people preferred to spend their time looking for work rather than having a skills assessment. The guidance counsellors also provide group sessions of career guidance lasting up to three weeks, and 'deep guidance' sessions which can last up to three months. The latter is a continuation of the work of the *MLs* for the over-25s. In Paris at the time of our fieldwork, about 7,000-8,000 job seekers were involved in the three-week group sessions each year, and about 300 benefited from 'deep guidance' activities.

Conclusion

In France, there is a wide access to career guidance for adults at various stages in their careers. A large number of different organisations are involved in the provision of career guidance for adults. These organisations specialise in providing services to different segments of the labour market. Young people in difficulty receive guidance at the ML and PAIO. Trainees receive guidance from AFPA. Unemployed people receive guidance from ANPE. *Cadres* receive guidance from APEC. Women returnees receive guidance from *Retravailler*. Employees at all levels and stages can take leave of absence to receive guidance through the skills assessment system from a variety of providers of their choice, funded by a levy on employers.

Many of the providers are *Associations*, non-profit social enterprises whose mission is to improve the access of individuals to suitable career opportunities and to provide professional career guidance. The system is built substantially around a series of quasi-markets. Providers compete to provide skills assessment services funded by employers, and to provide further guidance to unemployed people funded by ANPE. Furthermore, guidance is provided alongside the training provided by AFPA under contracts negotiated with the Ministry of Labour. The system as a whole is well resourced and meets the needs of large numbers of adults for career guidance. The concern with social inclusion, with the provision of social as well as vocational guidance to tackle the broader social problems of young adults in difficulty, and with the needs of special disadvantaged groups such as women returnees, indicates that the French model of the learning society in important respects corresponds more closely to that of 'personal development' rather than the narrow skills growth model observed in the British case study.

A key feature of the French system is its pluralism. This has the advantage of ensuring that each different segment of the labour market is serviced by specialised, skilled guidance professionals, who have an insight into the specific problems of that group. Its disadvantage is that there is an inequality in provision due to the different funding bases which apply, ranging from the well-resourced services provided for managerial and professional staff through APEC, to the rather more precarious position of the *Retravailler* organisation which provides services for women returnees.

SEVEN

The Netherlands

Introduction

In the Netherlands, as in the UK, there has been a trend towards the marketisation of guidance services – making a market of the market brokers (Watts, 1995). This has occurred in the context of central government policies of deregulation and decentralisation, together with attempts to reduce expenditure from the public budget. The Dutch government moved in the 1990s to restrict its role to providing a broad policy framework for guidance services. The services are now purchased by schools and *Regionale Opleidingen Centra* (Regional Training Centres – RTCs) in the case of young people and those adults in vocational education, and by local Employment Offices in the case of unemployed people. Contracts are awarded to second-tier Regional Guidance Centres and a third-tier, fully privatised National Careers Guidance Information Centre to support them. These moves have involved profound changes in funding arrangements, in the infrastructure of provision and in the profession of career guidance. A quasi-market has developed in which users now contract for services, and in which there is an element of public subsidy to stimulate demand.

Guidance has not been identified as a priority area in the Netherlands. In schools, career guidance is connected to the idea of citizenship; indeed, the motto of the Education Department is 'not for school but for life'. The general approach to guidance for adults in the Netherlands is informed by Article 9 of the European Social Charter which states that every citizen has the right to access to free guidance. The Dutch government ratified the Charter in 1978. However, in practice, 'every citizen' has been taken to mean every citizen who is either unemployed or in vocational education. Hence, guidance for adults is focused largely within the activities of the Employment Service and the RTCs.

The education system in the Netherlands is characterised by its heterogeneity. In a selective system, pupils' destinations are decided on in accordance with their performance. Hence, there were, until 1999, five types of secondary-school education that a pupil might attend:

- junior pre-vocational education;
- junior general secondary education;
- higher general secondary education;
- pre-university education;
- senior secondary vocational education.

In 1999, the first and second of these merged into one: 'pre-secondary vocational education'. Children with the lowest educational qualifications after completing primary education are assigned to schools in this sector; they then tend to go on to senior secondary vocational education. Those with average qualifications attend higher general secondary education (some will then transfer to senior secondary vocational education or to higher vocational education in the tertiary sector). The best qualified go to pre-university education, of whom a substantial number will progress on to higher vocational education or university.

The pre-secondary vocational education schools (ie the merged junior pre-vocational education and junior general secondary education schools) are neighbourhood-based. At the other end of the spectrum, the pre-university education schools are much smaller, more academic, élite schools that recruit on a national basis and enjoy a higher status than the other schools. About 90% of the institutions in senior secondary vocational education comprise large RTCs – in effect, community colleges that combine secondary vocational education with adult education – the remaining 10% in this sector being made up of agricultural and nautical schools. Overlaying this hierarchy, there are separate Roman Catholic, Protestant and 'neutral' institutions, in both the state and private sectors. The commitment to freedom of choice in religious education allows considerable leeway to schools in curriculum development, including approaches to guidance.

The state of the economy had been poor for some time by the early 1990s. Accordingly, active labour-market policies were developed aimed at increasing the numbers of individuals in the labour market with a basic qualification, and at increasing educational output in terms of higher qualifications. Added to this was a change in orientation to guidance for unemployed people, whereby more emphasis was put on individual actors taking responsibility for themselves and creating their own career trajectory. This led to the provision and accessing of more information, including the use of the internet, CD-Rom and cybercafés. It also prompted more one-to-one guidance for those regarded as 'furthest from the labour market' – that is, disadvantaged people least likely to find suitable employment on their own.

Marketisation, decentralisation, deregulation and welfare-spending reduction policies have resulted in changes in funding systems for adult guidance, for the infrastructure and for the role of the guidance profession. These, in turn, have had profound implications for the provision of adult guidance, for who provides what, and for issues of quality and equity. We will now explore these various issues in more detail.

Guidance in the education system

In 1993, legislation on changes in secondary education meant that careers education became more firmly rooted. Schools were obliged by law to provide some guidance for young people but the nature and extent of such guidance was not specified. Pupils aged 14 to 16 identified as 'difficult' (and their parents) were encouraged to sign a contract with their school or RTC whereby educational services were to be delivered, in essence, in exchange for attendance at classes, completion of work and a promise to 'do one's best'. The contract included a commitment on the part of the school to provide some guidance.

Two levels of careers guidance were available for school-age young people. First, schools were obliged to designate an existing member of staff to be the careers teacher, who was then given five to ten hours a week or more to organise guidance activities and provide advice to pupils. Second, schools could draw on the services and expertise of state-subsidised Regional Guidance Bureaux (*Adviesbureas voor Opleiding en Beroep* – AOBs – to be described in more detail later in this chapter). Set up in 1993, they provided labour-market information and could make introductions to companies for work placements. Guidance in the education sector tended to be focused in the first instance on the transition from primary education to one of the categories of secondary schooling. In a sense, those who opted for senior secondary vocational education (the RTCs, agricultural or nautical colleges) had already made their occupational choice by going there.

One of the effects of the introduction of the decentralisation policy was that schools were given a block grant, rather than the previous arrangement of a set of earmarked funds for capital projects and various activities. The purpose was to enable schools to be more responsible for the quality of their educational and vocational services by using their resources to best effect. Schools were thus rendered free to make their own decisions about the extent to which they made use of the second-line services provided by the AOBs, or relied on their own front-line services. Combined with the introduction of output-funding arrangements, this free choice was intended to have the effect of improving quality (although quality was not defined). It was in the school's own interest to ensure that pupils enrolled on the most appropriate courses for them and hence qualified, in order to release further funding.

One immediate effect of this new set of arrangements was to make the cost of second-line guidance services more transparent. In the words of a former Inspector for Careers Guidance we interviewed:

> "Now that schools have to pay for guidance, having been used to having the services in a sense for 'free' (ie paid centrally), they see what it costs! They say 'Oh gee, does it cost!'"

As a result, many schools chose to rely more on their own careers teachers (even though training in guidance was not compulsory for them), rather than buy in expertise from the AOBs, whose guidance staff were trained and qualified professionals. Schools found the cost of the latter unattractive, compared to using their in-house staff. Some RTCs set up their own internal expert bureaux to help young people identify their abilities, being encouraged to do so by the introduction of the output-related financing policy.

At the same time as the decentralisation of school budgets, the direct resourcing of the AOBs by the state began gradually to be phased out, over a number of years. In effect, their budget was given to the education sector and the employment service, which could then choose whether or not to buy the services they required from the AOBs. In turn, the AOBs were required to generate their own income on the market, principally, of course, through selling their services to their two main customers – schools and the Employment Service. In so far as these services were provided free to clients at the point of delivery, this represented the introduction of a quasi-market based on publicly funded services contracted out to the AOBs and other new-entrant providers. In so far as the AOBs were able to sell their services directly to their clients, an open market for guidance was developed.

Regional Training Centres

Regional Training Centres, the 'higher vocational schools', are of particular interest to our concerns because, as community colleges, they provide education for adults as well as for young people. There are about 50 RTCs in the Netherlands, made up of amalgamations of schools in an area. For example, in the case of De Leijgraaf Community College, one of the smaller ones, eight schools merged to produce an institution of about 300 teachers, 100 other staff and about 5,000 students. Some colleges have as many as 25,000 students. The RTCs were originally funded according to the number of students on the books; that has changed to a basic amount received on registration, followed by more when a student qualifies.

As community colleges, the RTCs provide vocational education in a wide range of subjects for young people and adults. Adult students may be asked to sign a similar contract with the college as young people, based on the same law. In fact, there are three contracts: between the student/pupil and the college, between the student/pupil and the work-placement employer, and between the college and the employer. The contract between the student/pupil and the college includes a commitment on the part of the RTCs to provide career guidance; through this route, adults in the education system have an entitlement to guidance services. However, the situation is complex, as the entitlement for adult students can come through a number of routes. While full-time students have their entitlement direct from the college, those in the dual system on day release, and those working and studying on a part-time basis, have their entitlement to guidance services from their employers. Moreover, migrants have access to guidance from central and local government. Refugees with the appropriate level of education can attend community colleges for a 'newcomers' trajectory' under the auspices of the municipality; this includes basic guidance.

The adult student population in community colleges is extraordinarily diverse. The main student body is made up of 16 to 21 year olds in full-time secondary education, but adult students are integrated up to any age. In effect, what is on offer to them is a second chance at vocational and general secondary education. Almost all the courses are certificated and funding for the lowest-level courses has been cut.

The head of one community college described the provision of guidance services in his community college to us in the following terms:

"Guidance is delivered in a number of ways. In the first instance, it is integrated into the work of all teaching staff. In other words, teachers are obliged to raise and address guidance issues in the way that they teach. The RTC then also has trained specialists working on a student service desk. They are there to address the difficult or specialist cases. Finally, there are careers teachers who have a normal teaching load for half the time and act as counsellors for the other half. They tend to be teachers who just happen to be interested in the area. Some will have followed a training course in guidance but not all. They are encouraged to undertake training, however, and it is the policy of the head of department that they should."

Colleges have a financial incentive to retain students, in order to encourage them to progress on to other courses within the college, but only if they are likely to complete the course and qualify. Hence, good guidance services are in the interest of the college. The marketisation policy is based on the assumption that the market will enhance quality; if the student is not impressed by the standard of provision at the college, he or she may go elsewhere. Hence, competition is set up between the RTCs.

RTCs seek to enhance their income from other sources, the ESF being one option. ESF tends to be used for short projects for special groups – for example, Moroccan youngsters. However, there are difficulties in that there is a heavy administrative load attached to such funding, and a fundamental incompatibility between the government structural funding system and the ESF's annual accounting mechanism. The latter pushes RTCs towards hiring staff on a short-term basis. This is seen as attracting less qualified people and hence compromising on quality, thereby putting the college's competitive edge at risk. According to the head of a community college: "The ESF doesn't repair what the state neglects". Hence, colleges have to look for other income-generation strategies to supplement their income. Alternatives include offering bespoke courses to employers, such as language courses for migrant workers on the shop floor, and working with the Employment Service's own colleges for unemployed people.

Boards of community colleges have tended historically to be made up of worthy local citizens, but one of the effects of marketisation has been to highlight the need for RTCs to network effectively with the local labour market. As a consequence, local burghers are slowly being replaced on college boards by figures from the business community.

Similarly, there are attempts to modernise the colleges through management training for senior staff.

Guidance in the employment service

The Dutch programme of decentralisation, deregulation, marketisation and cost-cutting have extended right through the organisation of the Employment Service, which is now managed by a tripartite Central Employment Board made up of representatives of government, employers and trades unions. In the past the Central Employment Board had a firm control on the activities and *modus vivendi* of its regional branches, whereas now it sets only the broad parameters for the delivery of services. Local and regional employment offices are therefore relatively independent in how they go about delivering services within the national policy framework and the national and regional infrastructure. The Central Employment Board sets annual tasks for each region and output funding is related to the achievement of targets for placing job seekers. In 1996, decentralisation was taken one stage further; earmarking within budgets for activities such as guidance ceased. Individual employment offices now have even more freedom to decide how to use their devolved resources to deliver services effectively, including how to organise guidance services, how much to spend on career guidance, and whether or not to buy services on the market.

Hence, local offices now have autonomy in how they provide guidance services to those unemployed clients who they feel would benefit from them. For example, the Employment Service has traditionally employed its own psychologists for guidance work. These tend to be highly trained and oriented towards psychometric testing. However, local offices can now choose between using their own psychologists, and/or buying in services from the AOBs or from commercial providers. In effect, local employment offices have to decide whether it is more cost-effective to continue to employ their own psychologists or to buy services on the market.

Part of the agenda of central government was to reduce the budget of the Employment Service. Hence, the registered unemployed were divided into four categories:
- 'easy', placeable people;
- those who need a basic trajectory;
- those who need a more complex trajectory;
- the 'unemployable', that is, those who cannot be placed because

they have too many problems, such as drug addiction or a lack of social skills.

The logic of the four categories is that they represent each group's 'distance from the labour market', with the first category being the shortest distance away and the fourth category the longest. It is the Employment Service that decides who belongs in which category.

The fourth group, however, are now regarded as the responsibility not of the Employment Service but of the municipality. Technically, they have ceased to be 'unemployed'. It is the job of the municipalities to prepare them for reintegration, whereupon the Employment Service resumes responsibility for their insertion into the labour market.

It was also argued that those 'nearest' the labour market (ie the most 'placeable') did not need the help of the Employment Service. Indeed, only 5% of those in this category secured jobs through Employment Service offices. Given the growing demand for a 'flexible workforce', commercial placement bureaux have moved in and taken over some of the work formerly done by the Employment Service for people in this category.

Hence, groups at both ends of the continuum were in effect removed from the Employment Service, which was left with just the two intermediary groups. Much of the emphasis in the approach to service delivery for these two groups has been on training and guidance; the Employment Service has its own training schools to develop the employability of its clients.

Historically the traditional external supplier of guidance services was the local AOB, which was paid centrally for supplying expert services both to local employment offices and to schools and colleges. However, the true cost of their professional services was revealed by the marketisation process, and some local employment offices have eschewed these services in favour of cheaper, independent suppliers.

Marketisation and the adult guidance infrastructure

In a major initiative in the context of the policy of reducing public funding, the Ministries of Education (*Ministerie van Onderwijs, Cultuur en Wetenschappen* – OCW) and Employment (*Ministerie van Sociale Zaken en Wekgelenheid* – SZW) brought together their respective in-house guidance activities and developed a more streamlined approach. The aim was to provide an infrastructure for a back-up service to support the front-line practitioners in schools and colleges (the careers teachers and school bureaux) and in the Employment Service (the placement officers and psychologists). This has inevitably created a different set of conditions within which the AOBs operate. It also led to the dismantling of some institutions and the creation of others to provide second and third-line support services.

Regional Guidance Centres

The policy changes in the education and employment services have spelled trouble for some second-line providers, in particular the Regional Guidance Centres. AOBs were originally set up in 1993 on a regional basis, and were funded directly by the state as not-for-profit organisations to provide services on request to schools, colleges and the Employment Service. They were formed through mergers of previously independent career guidance bureaux, contact centres of education and work, and regional bureaux for the apprenticeship system. AOBs have felt the full force of marketisation. Their budgets for guidance work were transferred to front-line organisations which could then choose whether or not to buy services from the AOBs. As the centres employed trained professionals, their services were regarded as expensive. AOBs had to fight to survive; they needed to become competitive and to diversify their sources of income. Many bureaux soon found themselves in financial trouble. Indeed, by 1999, only 12 of the original 16 still survived, some of which had taken over those that had gone bankrupt. AOBs had also lost one fifth of their total staff; some individuals made redundant had set up their own private companies and were directly competing with AOBs by offering their services directly to schools at cheaper rates.

One of the difficulties facing AOBs has been that they have never developed services for employers; as a consequence they are missing a small but significant market for guidance work. In recent years employers have sought more flexibility in their workforces, especially given the changes in work practices caused by developments in new technologies. To make entire sections redundant would soon give a company a poor reputation as an employer. A response by some companies in this situation has been to invest in the exit strategies of their employees. This may mean making a considerable resource available for training and vocational guidance, to ensure that those being made redundant are prepared for and relocated in employment that is acceptable to them. That way, the company retains its reputation as a good employer and can continue to hire and fire with complete flexibility. It is not, however, the AOBs that have been chosen to provide this service for redundant employees. Rather, it tends to be small private-sector providers that have benefited.

Hence, many regional bureaux increasingly look to European funding to supplement their income, and use their contacts with schools to participate in projects which include some guidance work. Newly-privatised providers at local, regional and national level also make considerable use of EC programmes for guidance activities, making the Netherlands one of the largest recipients of EC co-funding for guidance and guidance-related activities.

The National Careers Guidance Information Centre

In the late 1980s, in keeping with government policy, the Ministries of Education and Employment privatised elements of their guidance services and set up an entirely new organisation, the National Careers Guidance Information Centre (*Landelijk Dienstverlendend Centrum –* LDC), to provide third-tier guidance services. It brought together staff from the Department of Information within the Ministry of Education, and the Department of Occupation and Job Profiles in the Ministry of Employment. The LDC was originally based within the Employment Service; however, in 1992 it was formally established as a not-for-profit foundation. The newly privatised LDC was then relocated from The Hague to Leeuwarden in Friesland, in the north of the Netherlands, as part of a government policy of office dispersal. The LDC has a contract with its sponsor ministries to develop programmes for careers teachers and materials for young people. While originally its work focused on developing an information base on educational and occupational opportunities, it came to be more concerned with developing theoretical frameworks and methodologies.

The LDC received an annual subsidy of 5.5m guilders per annum. It had been calculated that its running costs came to 8.5m guilders; the shortfall was to be met through a combination of cost saving and income generation. In the context of marketisation, the privatised LDC redefined its role from being state-subsidised to becoming more or less a commercial agency with some public-sector contracts.

Originally the LDC had very much a civil-service ethos; indeed 60% of the original employees were civil servants from the two sponsor ministries. However, the move to Leeuwarden was not attractive to many of the ex-civil servants; some left at that juncture and new staff were recruited. Unlike many other services that were privatised at the time – such as the pilot services at Rotterdam and the registration of landowners, both of which went into the red – the LDC initially thrived in the marketplace.

One of the senior managers of the LDC explained: "We are not driven by maximising profit but by cost-cutting, developing a methodology that the market demands". An example of this approach was a magazine created by the LDC for schools. Previously, this had been delivered free, and even though the content was informative, it was not widely used (indeed, LDC staff found unopened boxes of the magazine at various schools). The LDC now began to charge a subsidised rate for the publication, in the belief that having to pay for it increased its value to the consumer. The LDC also reduced the numbers produced; hence it was now both generating income and incurring reduced costs. It addition, it revolutionised the magazine's appearance to make it more competitive with those produced by, for example, the financial services sector anxious to access the youth market. According to our respondent in the LDC: "You can now be seen with it and still be cool".

The main work of the LDC, however, has been producing structured information and analyses on education and the labour market, in particular forecasting which occupations are likely to grow and decline, and providing information about qualifications and skills needed for those occupations likely to expand in number. There is clearly a market for such information from the AOBs as well as from schools, the RTCs and the local employment offices. The matching of education and occupational profiles with labour-market data is technically sophisticated work, for which the LDC has developed new methodologies. It has also categorised occupations into groupings that can be used in the guidance sessions provided by front-line services.

The LDC is another part of the guidance infrastructure in the Netherlands that is involved in a considerable number of EC co-funded action programmes, in this case mostly projects under LEONARDO DA VINCI. This is beneficial both to the development of transnational linkages and to the enhancement of the LDC's reputation at an EU level, although as always there is an opportunity cost and a heavy administrative burden attached to EC co-funded projects.

Guidance counsellors

As a result of deregulation, guidance is now more integrated into other activities such as personal development, outplacement and continuing education and training. This has led to difficulties for traditional practitioners from the Employment Service, who previously tended to focus on job matching; they have had to broaden their range of activity. According to Meijers (1995, 1997), while deregulation adversely affected the old infrastructure and weakened power relations connected with guidance, it cleared the way for a reorientation of the entire field. This included:

- a shift in the content of guidance (from testing and matching to career learning);
- changes of organisational context (from an isolated activity to an integral part of the education or placement process);
- new patterns of cooperation (from the 'xenophobia' of psychologists and careers teachers to cooperation with human resource management and human resource development professionals).

Guidance counsellors have clearly had to adapt to a much-changed world. They have been forced to reorient themselves with regard to the 'added value' of guidance, and to sell themselves. They also have to operate in an increasingly competitive market.

According to the chairman of the Dutch Federation of Careers Teachers (*Nederlandse Verniging van Schooldekanen* – NVS), students are expected to become more autonomous in the learning process, and the primary process of guidance teaching is now seen to be the responsibility of subject teachers. They are expected to make links to the workings of the labour market in their treatment of the curriculum, whatever the subject. Hence, the role of the traditional guidance teacher is now to be responsible for organising the process. However, inspection of career education tends to be limited to schools having to demonstrate that adequate hours have been allocated to the task by designated careers teachers. One of the effects of marketisation has been to reduce the use made of the AOBs. Careers teachers are more heavily relied on for service delivery. However, training is still only regarded as desirable rather than as a requirement for such staff.

The Netherlands Institute of Psychologists (NIP), the professional association for qualified guidance counsellors, has had to change its role in the context of these changes. It has shifted from developing instruments to being a channel of communication about instruments and information, according to a senior member of the Institute we interviewed. Indeed, NIP now charges commercial and public-sector organisations for advice on new instruments, products or methods. Whereas previously there was a 'gentleman's agreement' between NIP and the publishers of diagnostic tests that the latter would only sell intelligence tests to those who had studied how to use them, the rapid expansion in numbers of people calling themselves counsellors has led to this agreement being compromised. They are now sold, for example, to school counsellors who may have had no training at all.

Indeed, the creation of a market has led to the growth of many independent providers seeking to sell guidance services to schools and other clients. This has led to under-cutting on price. Some AOBs have been reported to have reduced the hourly rate of their professionals from 160 to 140 guilders in order to maintain or improve their market position. Whereas membership of NIP may be a badge of quality, it is also an indicator of price; some consumers prefer to pay less qualified, cheaper counsellors. As a consequence, professional bodies have been in crisis and there have been growing concerns among their members about two key elements in the marketisation process: quality and equity.

Quality

One of the effects of the marketisation of guidance services in the Netherlands has been to weaken the influence of NIP, the professional association for qualified guidance professionals. NIP members used, for example, to be involved with the maintenance of quality standards, through inspections of guidance services. As one senior member of NIP explained:

> "I was a member of a 'quality audit team' that looked at personnel
> and counselling in colleges. All these merged organisations (RTCs)
> are supposed to provide some personal guidance and counselling to
> their students but in our inspection we found only three that were
> providing counselling. You need specialist tutors."

However, these inspections no longer happen, and the inspection service has been dismantled. The AOBs have had to concentrate on their fight for survival and have not been a focus for the development and overseeing of quality standards. The LDC has been removed from the day-to-day delivery of services and does not have a direct role in relation to inspection of quality or the maintenance of standards. It is up to schools and colleges and local employment offices themselves to consider quality issues for guidance as part of their more general quality-control concerns. This does not create an environment for clear and transparent monitoring of quality standards.

Moreover, there has been such an expansion in demand for counsellors that colleges have seen a gap in the market for short courses purporting to provide adequate training to become a counsellor. The same senior member of NIP quoted earlier expressed concern about the impact of this trend on quality in the following terms:

> "More of the colleges are now offering training courses in counselling, in order to make money. They try to get people in from schools, for example, who want to provide their own counselling to students. The colleges offer them a course of, for example, just 12 days. The college's prospectus then says that when you have finished the course, you are allowed to enter the UBA register. The register is for people who have had four years of higher education and a practice placement of 10 months in specialist institutions for psychological diagnostics! The UBA has a quality standard – you are not allowed to enter the register without it! What these colleges are saying in effect is: 'Come here and do this 12-day course on psycho-diagnostics' (everyone who does counselling in schools and so on wants to know how to handle tests), 'pay these rather high fees, and then you are entitled to do everything that someone who has had four years of training and 10 months of practice can do!' They say: 'There will be a certificate at the end of 12 days, and with that you can ask to be accepted on the register.' Of course, anyone can ask, but you won't be accepted. This is one of the effects of marketisation."

In short, marketisation has been accompanied by the dismantling of inspection procedures, the expansion of demand for counsellors and hence of training courses for them, and the decline in influence of the professional associations that were the guardians of quality. At the same time it is clear that what goes on in the name of counselling is much more diverse. Those concerned with psychometric testing are criticised for their distance from the labour market. Those with an intimate knowledge of educational requirements for occupations are criticised for their lack of client-centredness. It is too early to say what effect the attempt to integrate guidance into other activities such as education will have on quality of provision, but it is also the case that mechanisms for measuring quality do not exist beyond inference from course completion and placement rates.

Equity

Until now there has been no appetite in the Netherlands for monitoring by gender, ethnic origin or disability, so it is difficult to evaluate the impact of the marketisation measures on groups that are disadvantaged in the labour market through discrimination or other factors. However, the categorisation of unemployed people into four groups has the advantage of inhibiting the extent to which local employment offices might be motivated by placement targets to focus on the easy-to-place. This has certainly not been avoided elsewhere.

The dilution of quality among professionals through the growth in short courses, the demise of inspection and the undermining of the professional associations are likely to have a particularly deleterious effect on the most disadvantaged clients. Migrants and women returning to the labour market have been identified as needing specialist help, for which counsellors with professional training are needed. Before marketisation, the local employment offices would have passed these clients to the AOBs for specialist advice. This is now less likely to happen.

The increased emphasis in guidance on accessing information to enable the 'actor' to make informed decisions about their own lives is another element in the changed landscape of guidance counselling that will have deleterious effects on equity. Those with language difficulties, older unemployed workers and women returnees will be disadvantaged under a system that encourages autonomous approaches to creating trajectories and securing placement. Articulate middle-class clients in schools, colleges and among the unemployed are most likely to benefit from this new approach.

The quasi-market means that those individuals seeking guidance who have few resources will purchase it from the cheaper, and therefore probably less-qualified, supplier. Without the protection of membership of a professional association, there will be no guarantee of standards and no comeback in the event of bad advice.

European projects have become a focus for work with disadvantaged groups and here it is the client-centred personal development model of guidance that is on offer, again integrated into other activities such as training. However, this represents but a small part of the overall system.

Conclusion

In the Netherlands, there have been profound changes in the way that adult guidance services are organised and in the nature of guidance activities that are now supported. The emphasis has been on integration with other activities. The marketisation of guidance services has led to shifts away from client-centred guidance to more labour-market-orientated work, albeit rooted within an educational curriculum or a back-to-work trajectory for unemployed people. Guidance for employees is on the increase, and some of those made redundant are offered the choice of either a redundancy package or outplacement guidance by their employers. The marketisation of guidance and the need to generate income have led to the Netherlands becoming (proportionately) one of the biggest contractors for European co-funded programmes such as LEONARDO DA VINCI.

In the rhetoric of the EC, we see economic competitiveness underpinning economic, social, and teaching and learning policies, but with some space for 'special groups' who need particular projects and guidance to steer them away from limiting choices. The range of special groups has been expanded from women to include a broad raft of equality dimensions. For such disadvantaged target groups, the personal-development model of guidance is accommodated within funding for positive action projects. This is partly in order to combat social exclusion, but with an ultimate aim of adding to the stock of human resources.

The dominant model of the learning society in the Netherlands, however, is the skills growth model. A distinction is made between unemployed groups according to their distance from the labour market, and the kinds of guidance activity allowable vary accordingly. Guidance is now integrated into learning activities and back-to-work trajectories. The commercial sector has developed rapidly in response to the marketisation of services and to funding opportunities available from the EU. We see here, then, two models in operation simultaneously.

EIGHT

Italy

Introduction

This chapter draws on our fieldwork to describe the Italian guidance system, which, curiously, is largely characterised by its absence, in the sense that there is little or no state provision of guidance for either adults or young people. This is surprising, given the high level of public expenditure in Italy relative to GDP. However, the Italian state is a 'weak state'; it is highly decentralised, with significant autonomy given to regional governments. In the past, more attention has been given to the provision of subsidies to state-owned industries and to setting up regional resource centres to support small businesses than to reducing frictions in the labour and learning markets. Although every region in Italy has an Employment Agency, there is no national coordination, nor are there any government programmes for adult guidance. Now, however, as elsewhere, the old system of a 'job for life' is breaking down and new needs are emerging. Many organisations, including the local authorities, the trades unions, private companies and professional training centres, see a new demand for guidance developing and are becoming more active in the field. However, access is patchy and varies enormously from one region to another. Some regions cope very well with disadvantaged groups, while others provide virtually no special services at all.

The guidance system in Italy is strongest in the autonomous regions of the north. This is because the autonomous regions are well funded and have greater discretion over the use of their resources than other regions. Other northern and north-central regions such as Lombardy, Piedmont, Emilia Romagna and Tuscany also have well developed guidance services. Piedmont, in north-west Italy, is one of the more active regions in this regard, and we focused our case study there. In the Province of Varese, there is a coordinated policy linking guidance training and employment policy, stimulated by the decline of the local aircraft industry. Our interviewees there stressed that guidance must be strongly linked with other services such as training and local authority active-employment policies.

A rigid labour market

A characteristic of the Italian labour market is the presence of powerful trades unions that have been able to promote highly protective labour legislation. This has led to extreme inflexibility in the labour market, employers incurring high costs for hiring and laying-off staff (Dell'Aringa and Lodovici, 1997). Italian employees who are threatened with unemployment are protected by a special scheme, known as the CIG (*Cassa Integrazione Guadagni* – Wage Supplementation Fund), which covers employees on 'temporary' lay-off. The CIG is a peculiarly Italian scheme designed to support temporary lay-offs from large companies. The 'ordinary fund' (CIGO) covers short-term lay-offs or reductions in working time for up to six months, while the 'special fund' (CIGS) covers longer-term lay-offs due to company restructuring for up to two years, although in practice it can last for many years. Employees can be laid off and receive 80% of their earnings while still formally in employment, and can later be taken back into employment by their company. During the 1990s, the CIG has covered the wages for the equivalent of over 200,000 workers per year.

Permanent jobs in the public sector are accessed through a public examination that is held every year or so, depending on public-sector needs. Between these selection procedures, whenever there is a local labour shortage, unemployed people can be hired from the employment office on a temporary basis for a period of up to three months. The longer one has been unemployed, the greater the chance of being hired under this scheme.

Local employment offices (Ufficio Provinciale del Lavoro e della Massima Occupazione – UPLMO) provide support for workers who are unemployed. The UPLMO have a legal monopoly of labour-market transactions. Private job agencies, such as Manpower, are forbidden to make job offers in Italy, and are required to put all their job placements through the UPLMO. However, the local employment offices are not very successful; only 5% of job placements in Italy are made through them. The great majority of placements are made through personal contacts and informal networks. Three categories of unemployed people can be identified:

* the 'ordinary unemployed' (*disoccupata ordinario*), first-time job seekers, or people with only a short period of work experience;
* the long-term unemployed, who have been out of work for 24 months;

- the temporarily or 'mobile' unemployed, on the *Lista Mobilità* (see below), who have been made redundant from commercial companies over a certain size.

Social assistance payments to the 'ordinary' unemployed range from 300,000 lira to 1,500,000 lira (about £100 to £500) a week, depending on family circumstances. Eligibility for these payments lasts for six months, after which the unemployed person has an interview with a counsellor to see if they are really looking for work. A peculiar feature of the system is that school-children can register at the unemployment office when they reach the age of 14. When they leave school at 16, they count as long-term unemployed and hence their employers are eligible for a wage subsidy.

Workers who are affected by collective dismissals under redundancy agreements negotiated as part of a restructuring programme in larger companies are placed on a social welfare programme known as the 'mobility list' *(lista mobilità)*. Redundancies from large companies are organised by agreement between the company, the state and the trades unions. Together, they decide who is to be made redundant and placed on the list. Listed individuals are supported on favourable terms while they look for work. By the mid-1990s, over a quarter of a million workers were receiving unemployment benefits through the list. They receive 80% of their previous wage for one year if they are under 30, for two years if they are under 40, and for three years if they are over 40. They can work for up to 20 hours a week and still receive benefits. Many of these individuals are taken on by local authorities, who are the employers that make most use of the list. In theory, listed people are meant to use their time to improve their skills and to look for work. In practice, many work in the black economy *(lavoro nero)*. The law obliges all people in 'mobility' to undertake guidance, but in practice the law is not enforced. The scheme also provides a source of support for small and medium-sized enterprise (SME) start-ups, since a person on the list can capitalise the unemployment benefit if they start their own new business. Employers who take people on from the list get a wage subsidy in the form of a tax refund.

The high cost of laying off workers, together with the support for temporary lay-offs, has meant that Italian workers in larger companies, and in the extensive public sector, are in a relatively well-protected position. This partly explains the absence of an integrated guidance service; those lucky enough to find employment in the large companies or state establishments experience not the 'death of career', but its longevity. There has therefore been little need for continuous career guidance in the Italian labour market. Nor has there been a substantial need for initial guidance in a labour market that still relies heavily on 'connections' rather than merit for job placement.

Nevertheless, pressed by the forces of globalisation, this situation is beginning to change and the rigidity of the system is starting to loosen at the edges. As the labour market becomes more flexible, the need for guidance is increasing rapidly. Into this gap, new third-sector guidance providers have begun to insert themselves (Borzaga and Chiesa, 1997). We looked at a number of these newly emerging organisations in the north-west Italian region of Piedmont. We found that newly emerging providers are characterised by their strong connections with local and regional government, and with local business interests, as well as by the high degree of involvement of their clients. In the case of so-called 'social cooperatives' (*cooperatives sociale*) that operate in the welfare sector, clients often become members of the cooperative organisation.

Social cooperatives

More than in most other European countries, Italy has a thriving cooperative movement (Earle, 1986; Bartlett, 1993). Cooperatives of both left and right can be found in most regions, but especially in the north, and in Emilia Romagna and Tuscany. Law 381 of 1991 provided special support for two types of 'social cooperatives':

- 'Type A' social cooperatives provide personal services to unemployed people and disabled people, and personal care for older people.
- 'Type B' social cooperatives aim to hire disadvantaged people, such as those with disabilities, ex-offenders and drug addicts undergoing therapy, and provide them with jobs and work experience.

Under the law, the cooperatives are required to employ at least 30% of the workforce from these disadvantaged groups in order to be classified as social cooperatives. Registered social cooperatives are exempt from the requirement to pay VAT and social-security contributions.

At the time of our fieldwork there were around 4,000 social cooperatives in Italy. They had grown rapidly as a bottom-up initiative because of the increasing extent and awareness of social problems such as drug addiction and homelessness, and because of the inability of local authorities to organise the provision of effective social and welfare services. As service providers, they had developed a reputation for being significantly more flexible than local authorities and more responsive to consumer needs. Despite receiving relatively low wages, the workers in the social cooperatives were regarded as being better motivated than public-sector employees. A recent study of working conditions in Italian social cooperatives has shown that this is primarily because employees share a set of values and are more orientated towards socially useful work and an improved quality of working life, rather than monetary rewards (Borzaga, 2000). In comparison to the public sector, it is likely that the quality of service offered by the cooperatives is higher. They may or may not provide a better quality service than private-sector providers, but on the whole the private sector does not find it profitable to operate in many of these fields of public welfare. Hence, social cooperatives fill a niche in the market in which they compete for contracts with local authorities against other cooperatives and private firms.

In order to gain a better understanding of how these organisations operate in the field of guidance services we carried out interviews in a number of social cooperatives in north-west Italy.

Orientamento Lavoro

Orientamento Lavoro had been established in Milan in 1986 specifically to provide guidance services to clients. Its original purpose was to provide services for women returners to work and to improve their position in the labour market. Although it had extended its scope beyond this, it still mainly provided services to benefit women. In collaboration with the local Employment Agency, *Orientamento Lavoro* selected clients from the *lista mobilità* and called them for an interview. For those that chose to make use of the service, a set of nine sessions was offered over a three-week period (36 hours in all), followed by three further sessions at monthly intervals. *Orientamento Lavoro* preferred to work with groups rather than individuals, although individual counselling sessions were also provided.

When the social cooperative was first set up, free office space was provided by the Commune of Milan, and the staff worked as volunteers without pay. Initial interviews were provided to clients free of charge. During its first year of operation the service was financed by a grant from the government of the Lombardy region, but subsequently a nominal charge of 50,000 lira (about £25) was introduced in the form of a membership fee. Members were able to use the library and receive advice on developing their CVs and other similar information and advisory services. After their initial interview, clients could pay for various other guidance services. Courses of various lengths were available, depending on how long the client had been out of the labour market; these were charged on an hourly basis. Other services offered included a skills assessment (*bilancio di competenza*) designed for people with previous experience of work.

Short courses were also available for women returning to work after maternity leave. These courses were usually based on the principle of group activities. A further service was the *laboratorio* for women working in the regional and communal governments. These 'laboratories' provided an opportunity for women to reflect on their professional identity, the structure of the regional organisations within which they worked and the opportunities available to them. The region wanted to understand better why women did not take up training opportunities as often as men. It was found that women had relatively poor access to information, and that training provision was often used by employers as part of a reward system. In addition, *Orientamento Lavoro* provided guidance services for female prisoners and ex-offenders.

Centri Orientamento Retravailler and Donne e Formazione

Orientamento Lavoro was a member of the Italian network of *Retravailler* associations known as 'CORA' (*Centri Orientamento Retravailler*), which grouped together the 26 associated *Retravailler* centres in Italy (see Chapter Six for an account of *Retravailler* in France). Some of these were set up as private-sector organisations, while others were social cooperatives and yet others were public organisations. In addition, CORA had developed a project for women who had been on the CIG scheme in the centre and south of Italy; it also involved disadvantaged groups, including young adults in difficulty, disabled people and prisoners. About 3,000 women were included in the project in 1993/94, some of whom had been in CIG for many years (one for as long as 18 years).

CORA was a member of an umbrella group, *Donne e Formazione* (DF), which, as its name suggests, provided guidance and training services mainly to women returnees. DF was a consortium of organisations that included among its members:

- *Pari e Dispari* – a research company specialising in equal opportunities for women;
- *Gender* – a social research cooperative specialising in research on women and work;
- ACIPA – the training body of the small business and artisans' association CNA (*Confederazione Nazionale dell'Artigianato*);
- *Donna Lavoro Donna* – a women's training organisation.

One of the DF's activities was a project funded by the region of Lombardy to help unemployed people over 35 years old. The project began with a questionnaire, carried out by *Gender*, of the needs and competencies of local unemployed people, together with some research on the different kinds of businesses in the area. Appropriate interviews and courses were then offered to the clients. At the time of our fieldwork the project had ended, but two permanent workers had been established to carry on the work. The project also gave grants to people who wanted to set up cooperatives.

ORSO

Another social cooperative, ORSO, based in Turin, provided guidance services mainly to young adults. ORSO aimed to provide guidance services to promote transitions to work and to training, and promote the professional development of people already in work. It was one of the first social cooperatives to provide guidance services in the Piedmont region. Since its creation, ORSO had grown from its initial nine members (three worker members and six financing members), and by 1996 had over 60 members.

One of its initiatives was SAL (*Servizio Accompagnamento al Lavoro*). This was based at the Employment Department of the Commune of Turin and funded by the local authority. Created in 1987, the initiative was based on an idea developed by members of the Young Men's Christian Association (YMCA) who were concerned with finding jobs for young unemployed people. SAL provided opportunities for long-term unemployed people to undertake socially useful work, and provided job search guidance. Initial interviews were provided free of charge, and clients were then referred to a training course or to further guidance. ORSO also provided a service to companies to assist in placing surplus workers in new jobs. Outplacement services were relatively new in

Italy; in the past, the state had relied on the CIG and the *lista mobilità* to solve problems of labour relocation.

PromoLavoro

An example of another type of organisation linked to and supported by local business organisations in partnership with local authorities was *PromoLavoro* (the Novara Agency for Human Resources Outplacement and Development). Based in the town of Novara, mid-way between Milan and Turin, it had a staff of seven in 1996 – four senior and three junior. Founded in 1994 in response to the growing problem of unemployment in Novara, it was a private limited company that provided information, counselling and career development courses to its clients. According to the manager of the organisation, the advantage of being a private organisation was that *PromoLavoro* had much more flexibility than if it had been a public body constrained by the bureaucracy and hierarchy of the public sector in Italy. It was financed on an annual basis by the local Chamber of Commerce, the City Council and the Province of Novara to provide guidance services free of charge to unemployed people in the locality, as well as to employees seeking a change of career.

The organisation claimed a 30% success rate in assisting clients to find new jobs, compared to 5% for the local employment office. Its first contract was to work with the third category of unemployed people – those on the *lista mobilità* – but subsequently it had extended its range of activity to cover all categories of unemployed people as well as employees who wanted to change their job. *PrimoLavoro* had an agreement with the local UPLMO to provide guidance services, working in collaboration with the Navaro Employment Office and with access to its database. *PromoLavoro* offered guidance to individuals and groups on employment and self-employment, provided business start-up advice, conducted interviews, and ran short courses. It had an 'information room' offering information and documents, a computerised databank storing company information, a PC on which clients could prepare CVs and letters, and a telephone service.

New clients were offered an interview, attended an individual counselling session and had open access to the information room. These services were all provided free of charge to clients. However, in order to be eligible to use the service, a client had to be registered at the Labour Office (*Ufficio di Collocamento*), either in Novara or in a neighbouring commune. By 1996, 1,190 people had used the service out of 11,000 people registered in the locality. Access was open to all categories of unemployed people, including immigrants. There was no special programme for disabled people, but there were plans to develop one in later years. There were specific programmes for graduates and for young adults with less than two years' work experience. For the latter, training courses were provided in specific skills such as sewing, and further courses were being developed for people from the 'lists' in mechanics and office automation. Overall, about one third of clients succeeded in finding jobs. There were no formal evaluations; however, staff at *PromoLavoro* were of the view that its placement rate was much higher than the normal rate in the Province.

Centri di Iniziativa Locale per l'Occupazione

Centri di Iniziativa Locale per l'Occupazione (Centres for Employment Initiatives – CILOs) were another type of organisation that provided guidance and information services to people of all ages. CILOs had been established under regional laws, although in practice they were found mainly in Piedmont, Emilia Romagna, Abruzzo and Lazio. The target group for their activities was families with several members in search of employment, and single-parent families with school-age children. They were normally managed by private companies, by social cooperatives or by the public administration, depending on where and how they had been established. They provided courses on how to write a CV and on interview techniques. Every CILO had different projects and many of them worked with schools and enterprises.

The CILO in Rivoli was started in 1988, on the initiative of the director of the Economics Faculty at the University of Turin. It was set up in response to the growing problem of unemployment in Rivoli as Fiat began to cut back its orders from the local small businesses that traditionally supplied components. In 1996 about 5,700 people were registered as unemployed in Rivoli, out of a population of 52,000; the unemployment rate was 15%.

In 1995, the CILO was reorganised through a merger with the CILOs from the communes of Collegno, Grugliasco and Rosta. At the time of our fieldwork it provided services to a population of 160,000. Organised on a local level and supported by local business, it was one of the longest established CILOs in the region, employing six people – three from the cooperative and three from the region. It was managed by a social cooperative called *Educazione e Progetto* that had taken over the Commune Employment Office when it had been closed. It worked closely with the local branch of the small-business employers' organisation, CNA, to provide a package of work and training for unemployed people. In their first year of activity, they looked at individuals' labour-supply decisions and held meetings with the trades unions and employers' associations. After 1990, they started matching supply and demand for labour, using a database, and found that companies would prefer to use the CILO rather than the *Ufficio di Collocamento* (the Labour Office).

The CILO had also responded to specific needs through a number of projects. A shortage of nurses in the area had prompted a training programme to be set up; all 25 women who trained as nurses on the ESF co-funded course found a job. Another project involved persuading employers to provide temporary jobs to disadvantaged job seekers, in this case drug addicts and disabled people (subsidised for three months by the Commune), after which the employers could decide whether or not to take them on full-time. In 1992, the CILO had started re-qualification courses in crafts and in new technology sectors at various training centres.

Informagiovani

The guidance services on offer in Piedmont also included *Informagiovani*, which provided a variety of information to young people. Available all over Italy, most of these offices (over two thirds) were located in the north and centre of Italy. Most were run by social cooperatives. They were primarily financed by local Communes, and had offices in many towns in Piedmont. Some provided personalised counselling and educational guidance. They were designed to help young adults (rather like the PAIOs in France; see Chapter Six).

CODEX

Finally, CODEX was a social cooperative established in 1989 to promote self-employment through the provision of counselling and training. It was inspired by the French example of *Boutiques de Gestion*. Its initial focus was on training activities, but it later widened its activities to include the creation of enterprises and policies for the promotion of self-employment. It worked with and for the Province of Turin and the region of Piedmont, and had practically become a local economic development agency. Funded by the province and the region on a project-by-project basis, it had also succeeded in winning some co-funding for projects from the EU. One of these, a NOW project, was designed to help women set up in business. CODEX had also worked with an EC co-funded project called SPEC (Support Programme for Employment Creation) and had won an ADAPT project co-funded by the EU and the Ministry of Labour. It planned to establish advisory centres for women who wanted to set up small businesses, in which advice would be given on whether a new business idea would be feasible, and on the kind of support it would need.

Conclusion

In Italy, the emerging guidance system is much more fragmented and decentralised than elsewhere in Europe. It relies heavily on local initiative. But its principal characteristic, and lesson for policy makers elsewhere, is the way in which it demonstrates successful experiences of locally based guidance services supported by combinations of local authorities and local business interests. The practice among some providers of integrating users and practitioners in social cooperatives is an innovative approach to improving access for disadvantaged groups and building social cohesion from the bottom up. It reflects a desire to develop a more social approach to guidance, and is thus in keeping with the 'social learning' approach to the development of a learning society outlined in Chapter One. Operating on the basis of inclusion and mutuality, the Italian social cooperatives provide an important example of innovation in the provision of guidance services.

NINE

Germany

Introduction

Guidance services in Germany remain highly centralised and state-managed; there has been minimal marketisation of provision, certainly as far as statutory provision for young people is concerned. As elsewhere, there is a clear differentiation between the orientation of services for young people and for adults. Services for young people are focused in the employment service. They tend to be client-centred; young people are assisted by advice and information to follow their chosen preference in their initial transition from compulsory education or initial training to the labour or learning market. By contrast, services for adults tend to be tied into and affected by the drivers of other activities, as an adjunct to education and training services, or as part of integrated special projects for the disadvantaged. Their principal aim is to place the unemployed in the labour market, and so reduce the bill for unemployment benefit. The law promises free, objective vocational guidance for all, young people and adults. However, the accent in statutory provision for adults tends to be on guidance closely linked to finding a job rather than assisting the unemployed person to realise their occupational aspirations.

Several significant factors impact on the nature and provision of adult guidance services in Germany. First, reunification has had a substantial effect on the number and type of clients to whose needs the guidance services must respond. One of the key issues here is that qualifications acquired in the new *Länder* have not been recognised in the old *Länder*. In this chapter we draw, for comparison, on fieldwork in one *Land* in what was colloquially known as 'West Germany' and one in what was known as 'East Germany'. Second, the collapse of the economy in the new *Länder*, and the restructuring of the labour market more generally, are highly pertinent to the delivery of guidance services. For many East Germans, especially women, the experience of unemployment proved highly traumatic. These factors, combined with the availability of EC co-funding, have given rise to many training and employment projects for adults, incorporating a guidance element. There are now more third-sector providers integrating guidance into programmes of activities such as training and preparation for returning to work. Many of these projects are directed toward disadvantaged groups, such as women returnees, migrants or ethnic Germans 'returning' from Russia. This chapter examines the institutional determinants of service delivery in Germany, and the effects of recent contextual changes on quality and equity in guidance provision. We draw extensively on the work of our research partners (Chisholm and her colleagues), as well as our own fieldwork.

The legal base

An important background factor to understanding welfare services in Germany is the legal base that specifies who is responsible for what and to whom. As Chisholm et al (1997, p 2) explain:

> ... the idea of the *Rechtsstaat* – the just and legal state – is fundamental to the social formation and its legitimation in modern Germany. Based on the *Grudgesetz* – the Constitution – legislation specifies not only the rights and responsibilities of different levels of state and government but also of individual citizens vis-à-vis each other and in relation to state and community.

Article 12 of the *Grundgesetz* guarantees each citizen a free choice of an occupation, place of study or training and place of employment. The role of vocational guidance is to facilitate citizens in taking up that right.

However, this is interpreted differently for young people than it is for adults. The emphasis in the German guidance system is on fulfilling this statutory obligation to young people and assisting them to realise their chosen trajectory. Indeed, the very word for guidance in German (*Berufsberatungsdienst*) implies that the recipient is a young person. For adults, who constitute a significantly larger client group, guidance services are still overwhelmingly publicly funded, but tend for the most part to be linked with job seeking. Guidance takes place in the offices where unemployment benefit is processed. For those adults who are unemployed and receiving benefit, there is much more emphasis on job placement in the guidance offered; the individual is matched up with a suitable opportunity in the labour market rather than advised primarily in terms of what their ideal destination might be. The guidance services are located in the *Arbeitsamt*, the local employment service offices, and access to the services is linked to the process of claiming unemployment benefit. This provides a potential institutionalised tension and role conflict; at an institutional level, reducing unemployment statistics must be the main motivation of those providing the guidance, and this takes precedence over responding to the expressed desires of the client, should there be a conflict.

Given the number of unemployed people in Germany, the adult side of vocational guidance services – broadly defined – is much larger than that concerned with young people. For adults, the *Arbeitsamt* sponsors a range of short training courses designed to enhance their employability; guidance is linked to placement on these courses as well as to job placement. Indeed, the very words for guidance and for training are often used interchangeably, illustrating the link between the two. Benefit can be conditional on attending a short course designed to improve employability.

Until the 1990s, the state had a monopoly on placement. However, companies seeking senior executives who wanted to use the services of head-hunters successfully challenged this in the courts in August 1994. It was calculated in the early 1990s that about 1,000 such consultancy companies already existed in Germany, of which a third were well established (Ertelt et al, 1993, p 46). These companies tended to specialise in executive placement. In addition, a new wage subsidy was intended to encourage employers to recruit disabled people, and young people with special needs such as learning difficulties; because of this, the *Arbeitsamt* were permitted to put money into rehabilitation training institutions where staff were acknowledged as knowing the strengths and weaknesses of trainees better than *Arbeitsamt* staff, and therefore as being in a better position to place them. Despite these two erosions, the state has retained its near-monopoly on placement and on running guidance services that are attached to placement for unemployed people.

Institutional structure of statutory provision

Employment services

The main provider of guidance services in Germany is the Federal Employment Agency (*Bundesanstalt für Arbeit* – BfA). The BfA is funded by central government together with contributions from employers' and employees' organisations. These partners are represented on the governing bodies of the BfA at all levels. There is a head office based in

Nuremberg, 11 regional offices, 184 local offices and 640 branch offices (BfA, 1991) throughout Germany. The self-governing arrangement gives some autonomy to regional and local offices to determine priorities and direct funding to meet particular needs in their area. This might be to respond to changes in the local labour market or to invest in projects for disadvantaged groups. The local employment office, the *Arbeitsamt,* is where employers record vacancies and unemployed people register as job seekers. Employees seeking a new job or a change in direction can also use it. The *Arbeitsamt* covers the whole range of occupations and professions. In addition, they have responsibilities for promoting occupational training and re-training measures. *Arbeitsamt* employ employment counsellors and job placement officers. As Chisholm et al (1997, p 3) point out, Article 25 of the 1969 *Employment Promotion Act* specifies that: "Employment Office staff have an explicit duty to counsel clients and must offer objective and independent information and advice free of all charges".

An independent vocational guidance and counselling service operates as a separate sub-section of the BfA, known as the *Berufsberatungsdienst.* This service is geared primarily to young people making the transition from general education to initial training, although vocational education and training more generally are also promoted. While technically open to both young people and adults, in effect use of *Berufsberatungsdienst* is made overwhelmingly by the former. Chisholm et al (1997) note reports of a rising demand for such services among those abandoning their apprenticeships or degree courses and those becoming unemployed after completing their initial education and training (BfA, 1996).

To complement the work of the guidance services, there are vocational guidance and information centres, known as *Berufsberatungs-informationszentrum* (BIZ). The BIZ centres provide computerised information about occupations and the qualifications needed to be eligible to apply for them. Originally designed to assist young people to position themselves appropriately within the dual system, the centres also contain information on jobs and training courses and on how to apply for them. Information is available about the whole hierarchy of occupations and professions, including degree and postgraduate degree courses in Germany and abroad. Located in the *Berufsberatungsdienst* but also in shopping centres in towns and cities, BIZ centres are technically open to all people of all ages, but are used overwhelmingly by young people. For example, in the BIZ centre we visited in Bremen, 70% of users were reported to us as being under the age of 20. This reflects the pattern revealed in earlier research for all of Germany, which showed that 70% of users were under the age of 20 and that 64% were still at school (Hermanns, 1992). Information about vacancies is provided free on computer and details of courses throughout the EU can be accessed there on CD-Rom; the use of technology to present and display the information may contribute to the lack of use made of the BIZ by older people.

As Chisholm et al (1997, p 5) explain:

> The essential difference between the nature of mainstream provision through *Berufsberatung* (vocational guidance and counselling service) and the *Arbeitsvermittlung* (employment search service) *per se* is well caught by the different job titles of the counselling staff employed in each. In the former service, they are called vocational counsellors (*Berufsberater*); in the latter service, they are called employment counsellors and job placement officers (*Arbeitsberater, Arbeitsvermittler;* cf Ertelt, 1992, p 3n).

Education/training-based services

One area in which guidance and counselling have expanded in recent years is in services attached to education and training provision. Training centres run through Chambers of Commerce, Industry and Agriculture and through Adult Education Institutes provide the most in-depth services. According to Chisholm et al (1997), the Chambers are legally empowered to provide occupationally specific initial and further vocational training in cooperation with the Federal and *Länder* governments and employers. Counselling is oriented around occupational progress and career advancement. Counsellors and practising members of the Chamber who supervise the training courses act as mentors. Some will have had training in counselling.

There are over 1,000 Adult Education Institutes throughout Germany, financed by local and regional funds and by fees charged to participants. A wide variety of courses are offered on an open-access basis. In 1991, about 6 million participants took courses at these centres, 75% of whom were women (Ertelt et al, 1993, p 40). Guidance is provided as part of the activities of the Centres. According to Chisholm et al (1997, p 9):

> It is especially important for adult literacy/basic skills courses, for the 'second chance' students studying for secondary educational qualifications, and for the highly popular modern foreign language courses. The staff are all qualified educationalists, but they will rarely

hold formal guidance credentials or have attended special counselling training courses.

In addition to the provision offered by Chambers of Commerce and Adult Education Institutes, a range of organisations in the non-statutory sector provides vocational guidance linked to training. These include services provided by trades unions, professional associations, political and voluntary organisations, church-based bodies, charities and private enterprises. Some of the non-statutory provision is considered in the next section, drawing on our case studies. There is no specific federal legislation regulating this sector.

Non-statutory provision

The autonomy enjoyed by the self-governing regional and local *Arbeitsamt* enables the governing bodies to direct resources to address specific needs. Hence, investment can be made in projects that are geared towards a particular feature of the local labour market, such as a redundancy programme or an aspect of industrial restructuring, or resources can be allocated to projects that focus on the needs of specific groups. The regional or local *Arbeitsamt* budgets are a major source of funding for projects where guidance is integrated into training provision and back-to-work projects. However, the EC and federal or regional ministries (for example, the then Federal Ministry for Young People, Family, Women and Health) also underpin some activities oriented towards particular groups. There has been a significant growth in both third-sector and profit-making organisations seeking to target particular groups and offer counselling, and accessing these funding sources. We examined a number of such projects targeted at disadvantaged people, supported by organisations such as the *Arbeitsamt* or the EC, in two contrasting *Länder* of Germany: Bremen and Brandenburg. Bremen, an 'old' *Land* in the north of Germany, had many unemployed migrants, and was suffering the effects of redundancies in the shipyards in Bremerhaven. Brandenburg, a 'new' *Land* which includes the hinterland of Berlin, was dealing with major turbulence in the labour market and high levels of unemployment, especially in some urban areas following redundancies in the steel plants and the chemical industry, and also among women in rural areas. Both *Länder* have been recipients of migrants from Eastern Europe and elsewhere.

Koordinierungs- und Beratungsstelle Frau und Beruf – Zurück in den Beruf

The Coordination and Advice Bureau: Women and Work – Back to Work (ZIP) was a unique project; indeed, it had been called a model project. It was based in the city of Bremen. Originally set up in 1989, as one of 17 advice centres for women returnees funded by the (then) Federal Ministry for Young People, Family and Health, together with the *Land*, most of its funding at the time of our fieldwork (1996) came from the *Arbeitsamt*, the *Land* and ESF (Objective 3). It was aimed primarily at women returnees; however, its client group extended beyond this to include women recovering from illness, people who had been made redundant, and migrant women from Turkey, Latin America, Africa and Iran. ZIP was an example of an organisation where vocational guidance could be provided outside the state monopoly of the *Arbeitsamt* because the client group was identified as having special needs. ZIP also acted as a lobbying and networking organisation, campaigning for better opportunities for women returnees in further education, training and employment. The *Arbeitsamt* automatically referred women returnees to ZIP, which, in turn, ensured they were assisted to register as job seekers and claim any benefits to which they might be entitled.

The staff of four at ZIP was made up of graduates who had learned the counselling element of their work through practice and by consulting experts. Their main concern was political, to improve opportunities for women – hence the emphasis on lobbying as well as service delivery. ZIP saw about 1,600 women a year, 10% of whom were migrants; there was a target of 400 women per counsellor. Some sessions took place over the telephone. One respondent from ZIP described the difference between the service there and at the *Arbeitsamt*:

> "In Bremerhaven, they have only one woman to deal with women returnees. They get five to ten minutes.... The *Arbeitsamt* is trained to think about fitting women in to what is being offered. We spend an hour with women the first time they come. Women can come as often as they like. They never come more than five times. The exception is counselling for women who want to set up in business. Women feel different at the *Arbeitsamt*. It is an official office so you can't say everything you want to. There is a more familiar atmosphere here; it is more confidential. Women can talk about the black economy, childcare; they can show their face."

Increasingly, however, this client-centred approach, where the counselling process took as long as both sides felt was needed, was being compromised by growing insistence from funding bodies on the use of performance indicators such as throughput and placement rates.

Those working at ZIP saw a division between those who were close to and far from the labour market (reminiscent of the Dutch system – see Chapter Seven), with the *Arbeitsamt* providing services for the former, and ZIP and other projects responding to the needs of the latter. Resources were released to organisations such as ZIP to provide low-threshold guidance services, but their coverage across Germany and the extent to which all the disadvantaged groups such as women returnees were catered for varied over time and space (Clayton et al, 1997).

Berufsfortbildungswerk, Bremen

Founded 50 years ago, *Berufsfortbildungswerk (bfw)* had been set up with pump-priming money from the trades unions to deliver training in the context of rising unemployment. A national organisation with branches in each *Land*, this particular branch employed 65 people full-time and between 80 and 100 part-time, and provided re-training for employed and unemployed people. Training was delivered in industrial metals, commerce, travel agency work, computing, water delivery and waste disposal. Re-training took about two years and included work placements. The Chamber of Commerce provided certification for those who passed; the qualification was regarded as equivalent to that acquired through the much longer dual-training system.

The main sources of income were contracts from the Federal Employment Agency and the EC through the ESF, action programmes such as FORCE and (now) LEONARDO DA VINCI, and Community initiatives such as ADAPT. EC co-funding was regarded as increasingly problematic because of the level and detail of financial information required.

The Federal Employment Agency had previously paid a percentage of staff costs for guidance, but this had now stopped, according to our respondent. The EC would only pay for guidance for categories such as the 'old' (ie over 45) and for disabled people. Guidance was not supported for other unemployed trainees. Guidance staff at *bfw* tried to give guidance on demand or to arrange for trainees to have time out to consult *Arbeitsamt* guidance counsellors. Training was provided in applying for jobs and preparing CVs. Trainees with social problems were referred to social workers.

It was clear here that the organisation experienced difficulties in accommodating the different rules on offering guidance according to the funding source for specific trainees. In the words of our respondent:

> "Training should be organised to include guidance. The dual-training system is curriculum-dominated and doesn't deal with self-directed learning: how to find out what you need to know. There is very little time allocated for social and life skills or creativity in approach to the labour market. There shouldn't be this split between training and guidance. We run a course for 35 young people under 25 under ESF: they have to attend a training course for 35 hours a week. This is filled with practical work to pass the exam. They have to get guidance at the weekend or in their lunch hour. The training is very qualification-driven. Changes are needed in the organisation of training and the delivery of guidance to trainees. In the future we shall ask people to spend their own money on training. Because it is free, people don't value it."

Paritätisches Bildungswerk — Training and Counselling for Migrant Women

The *Paritätisches Bildungswerk* was a charitable, not-for-profit organisation that provided (inter alia) education and counselling for deprived groups. It offered a highly oversubscribed one-year course, funded by ESF and the *Land Bremen*, targeted at migrant women. Without advertising, there was a long waiting list of would-be participants. Originally aimed at Turkish women, the student body was now multi-cultural; women from eight countries attended, for all of whom German was their second language. Demand was increasing, particularly from women from Eastern European countries and from Turkey who were either newly arrived or (largely in the case of Turkish women) had grown up in Germany. Drop-out rates from school and apprenticeships were especially high among Turkish girls.

Staff at the *Paritätisches Bildungswerk* drew attention to the fact that the staff at the *Arbeitsamt* might not speak the first language of the migrant women, or understand the difficulties they faced in seeking employment. As one respondent said:

"*Arbeitsampt* don't employ migrants to work with migrants. Many of their problems are not acknowledged. Their qualifications from their home countries may not be recognised. There are perpetual problems encountered because of the legal status of migrants."

Indeed, some migrant women found themselves in a 'Catch-22' situation. State funding for unemployment benefit was restricted to the registered unemployed. However, in order to be eligible for benefit entitlement, an unemployed person must have contributed to the social insurance scheme for a minimum of 12 months within a specified time period preceding unemployment. This was problematic for newcomers such as migrants, and for women returnees and those who had been working below the threshold for eligibility to contribute to the social insurance scheme. Moreover, for a woman migrant, whether she was married to another migrant or to a German citizen could prove crucial to her eligibility to become a 'permitted' worker or job seeker. This 'permitted' status affected her entitlement to take paid employment and also her access to publicly funded language and training opportunities incorporating guidance. Migrant women had to prove their language competence and provide the equivalent of a school-leaving certificate. Hence the 'Catch-22': no social insurance contributions for those with no language skills meant no eligibility for training courses (including those in language skills) and no permitted status to work, and therefore no opportunity to contribute to social insurance. The *Paritätisches Bildungswerk* sought to break this vicious circle, but even here a working knowledge of German was needed and ESF Objective 3 co-funding demanded that students must be over 25 and registered as unemployed for at least a year. Only those who would eventually have eligibility to become 'permitted' were accepted at the *Paritätisches Bildungswerk*.

The course provided pre-vocational education and training for migrant women with a view to preparing them for further education or training. Work placement and guidance were included as significant elements of the course. There was a strong emphasis on personal development; the women were described as seeing the course as 'personal space'. Guidance was integrated into the classes and provided in response to personal need and opportunities.

Tertia Training and Consulting Ltd, Brandenburg

Tertia was a private-sector company set up in 1992, as part of a Germany-wide organisation which provided a range of services for unemployed people, including re-training, orientation and adult guidance. The company headquarters were in Bonn, and branches had recently been opened in Russia and Albania. A major source of income for the German branches was the *Arbeitsamt,* which paid on a per-capita basis for the registered unemployed to receive advice and training; 30-40% of clients were referred from the *Arbeitsamt.* Trainees and advisees tended to be long-term unemployed from Brandenburg in their mid-40s – the area had an unemployment rate of 24%. Many had been made redundant from the textile and steel industries. The training was regarded as high-quality and included a guidance element; employers recruited from the courses and only 1% 'failed'. Guidance clients, 90% of whom were women, tended to progress to further training. There was an overwhelming demand for services from *Tertia* from the 'Volga Germans' – Russians of German ancestry who spoke no German, but who, in the new political context, had exercised their right to return to their 'homeland' after their ancestors' departure to Russia 300 years previously.

The *Arbeitsamt* would only pay *Tertia* if 50% of the clients that they referred were placed in jobs at the end. This meant that securing a job was a key performance indicator for *Tertia*, alongside the numbers of participants who passed examinations, and the numbers given advice. With placement a key indicator, the company monitored vacancies from newspapers and through the computerised records of the *Arbeitsamt*; it was involved in the placement process itself. In order to improve employability, counselling went beyond career orientation to include advice on drug and alcohol abuse, family problems and so on. The amount of time spent on guidance for each client varied, in accordance with an assessment of his or her need. The disadvantaged and those with problems were targeted: "we would only turn away someone who was actually drunk". *Tertia* identified the needs of the 'Volga Deutsch' as especially time-consuming but the *Arbeitsamt* had not responded by identifying them as a special case.

The company believed that it could expand in Brandenburg; indeed, the market was such that there were now a few competitor organisations setting up in the area, offering similar services. However, of particular interest in the Brandenburg *Land* was the way in which a network of organisations had developed – some private-sector, some not-for-profit, all funded publicly rather than by clients – offering a hierarchy of training and guidance services on a trajectory back to the labour market. *Tertia's* position within this hierarchical network of organisations was critical because it took the most disadvantaged and passed them on to other organisations that could offer more than basic training and counselling. From here, disadvantaged job seekers could progress to more advanced and more labour-market-oriented training courses, vocational guidance sessions and work-placement opportunities.

Land of Brandenburg Agency for Structure and Labour Ltd, Potsdam

A third of *Tertia's* 'graduates' in Brandenburg went on to the Potsdam *Land* of Brandenburg Agency for Structure and Labour Ltd (LASA). This was a not-for-profit umbrella organisation (*Aufsichrativsivender*) responsible for administering the Ministry of Labour's budget for labour-market activities in the *Land* of Brandenburg. It also received ESF funding. As a coordinating agency or 'clearing house', it worked as a partner with the *Arbeitsamt*, but received no funds directly from it. There were no parallels to LASA in other *Länder*.

LASA's core activity was to create jobs (especially in rural areas where unemployment was high), to promote new structures in the labour market and to find measures to support them. Applications for funding for projects were made to the EC and government departments and then allocated to organisations that would deliver the projects. The target groups for projects were young people, women and former members of the Soviet Union's armed forces. It also managed ex-armed-forces property, estates and buildings.

LASA had been set up in 1992, amid concerns about the skill levels of East Germans. According to our respondent from LASA, a considerable amount of money had been spent on re-training East Germans, but much of it inappropriately. Despite being a PhD holder, he had himself, for example, been offered a low-level mathematics course. He and others had therefore founded LASA, responding to the opportunity created by the decision to invest in guidance to accompany, or ideally precede, re-training. Clients (both unemployed and employed) found LASA through advertisements and through referral from other agencies including the *Arbeitsamt*. It had five offices specifically for vocational guidance throughout the *Land*, employing 25 guidance officers and financed by the *Land* and ESF. Guidance was provided free to unemployed people and included advice on setting up enterprises and information about opportunities in the various schemes and projects that LASA coordinated.

The guidance workers at LASA had a variety of backgrounds but most were graduates. They had organised their own re-training as counsellors; however, most of their skills had been acquired on-the-job rather than through certificated courses. They collected information about the labour and learning markets and had access to the federal data system from Nuremberg on-line; LASA was well equipped with computing technology and had data on about 20,000 educational opportunities. Recent years had seen a swing from requests for information about jobs to those about education and training opportunities. This was in response to the decline in the labour market; in the view of our respondent, the only jobs in the area offering a living wage were branches of national or regional organisations such as banks that happened to be in Brandenburg.

There was no systematic evaluation of LASA or its activities, and no analysis of the destinations of the advisees; this was seen as problematic because of confidentiality. Demand from the public, the fact that word of mouth had been identified as the main referral source, and success in winning contracts, were interpreted by LASA as evidence of quality.

About 55% of those who came to LASA were women, of whom a majority were around the age of 45 and were unused to being unemployed. The next case study was a project to which many women in this category were referred by LASA.

Beratungstelle Frauen und Arbeitsmakt

The *Beratungstelle Frauen und Arbeitsmakt* was one of the organisations that came under the umbrella of LASA and was aimed at women in a rural area of the new *Land* of Brandenburg. Run on a shoestring, it was supported by ESF, the Ministry of Labour, the *Land* Department of Women and the local *Arbeitsamt*. It organised development projects for women, ran seminars, and gave advice and counselling on finance and enterprise, as well as on opportunities in education, training and the labour market. The main aim was to encourage women to be aware of their achievements, identify their skills, recognise their options, and develop action plans. It targeted long-term-unemployed women, women returnees and those seeking re-training. About 10–15 women a week sought guidance, some by telephone. The number of enquiries dropped off during harvest time and at Christmas.

The members of staff were all East Germans who had been unemployed themselves before joining the project. Although the Ministry paid for them to be re-trained, they had no specific training in guidance. There was considerable networking among this and similar projects across the *Land* and with relevant local organisations, but very little with the EC or potential transnational partners in other EU member states. It was the Ministry that handled contacts with the EC. The lack of networks with other EC member states, accentuated by the fact the staff had Russian rather than French or English as their second language, effectively cut off opportunities for participation in EC-funded transnational programmes, and therefore to accessing more substantial EC co-funding.

The particular problem faced by East German women clients is of special relevance to our concerns with lifelong learning and the learning society. They experienced trauma at becoming unemployed. As women in East Germany, working continuously and full-time throughout adult life had been the norm. Having to adapt to the West German model of gender relations at work and home was both unwelcome and difficult. Economic activity rates for women in the old *Länder* have been surprisingly low for a northern European state. In one survey in 1993, 60% of non-employed West German women reported that they described themselves as housewives, as opposed to only 8% in the East (Statistishes Bundesamt, 1995, p 480n).

At the same time, it was clear that these clients exhibited a more open approach to the prospect of re-training and assuming a new career than many made redundant from their occupations (so closely linked to personal identity) in West Germany. Indeed, the central planning system of East Germany had required them to do precisely this several times in a working lifetime. The project managers regarded them as facing fewer psychological adjustment problems in changing their career identities than West Germans, but as facing far greater practical problems in that their skills and qualifications were not recognised.

Quality

In Germany, the state monopoly of guidance services is being slowly challenged by a plethora of private and third-sector organisations that are integrating guidance into other activities. There are concerns that the professionalism of the state service may be undermined by the more amateur activities of new entrants where there is no regulation or control.

While guidance activities in the state sector are directly related to skills growth and the labour market, among many third-sector projects there is more of a personal development approach. The focus is on preparing people to return to work or training, by building up their skills and confidence to identify what direction they want to take and to be able to make appropriate decisions. For many, the outcome is to move on to another project or further training, more directly connected with the labour market.

When vocational guidance was the monopoly preserve of the *Arbeitsamt*, the Federal Employment Agency set its own standards. It has its own *Facholschule* (training college) that includes a labour-administration section. There is a three-year training course for guidance counsellors – both employment counsellors and vocational counsellors for youth – and further continuing training courses run in-house by the *Arbeitsamt* for qualified counsellors.

There is also a professional association for guidance counsellors in Germany, the *Berufsberaterverbaut*. This association is seeking to establish a profile for the vocational counsellor and to secure legal protection for it. Only those who have the qualification and update their training on a regular basis would, under these proposals, be allowed to practise. According to one of our respondents from the Berlin-Brandenberg *Landesarbeitsamt*:

> "Members of the professional association are perfectly happy with the activities of organisations such as voluntary associations and charities that deal, for example, with the special needs of Volga Germans. It simply wants to control the personal interview with clients for vocational guidance."

The freeing-up of the *Arbeitsamt* monopoly on placement has not led to a substantial growth in private-sector providers; the main increase in provision of guidance has come more from third-sector providers, integrating guidance with training and work-preparation courses. The lack of growth of the private sector in this field may be in part due to the poor state of the labour market. Again, our respondent from the Berlin–Brandenberg *Landesarbeitsamt* commented:

> "The Government hoped that in ending the state monopoly on placement, this would increase the placement rate, but the private sector is only really interested in placing those who are already employed. It facilitates movement between jobs but does not really

provide any improvement in the market placing the unemployed.... The profit potential for non-state sector providers is linked to the state of the labour market. If the economic situation improves, then there might be a growth in the number of organisations providing guidance and placement services."

As yet, then, quality of guidance is controlled in the statutory system, where the vast majority of adult guidance occurs. The problems of the labour market, the low economic activity rates of women in the old *Länder* giving rise to a steady stream of women returnees, and the growing migrant population, will inevitably lead to the consolidation and growth of third-sector providers. Yet this is where client-centred guidance is provided by people who are not necessarily trained to provide it, where no professional association is acting as a guardian of standards, and where performance indicators may focus on short-term measurable outputs rather than on processes.

Equity

While the law enshrines a national entitlement to adult guidance, what and how much is on offer from non-statutory providers varies considerably, according to where you live. There are variations between *Länder* because of the regional and local autonomy to determine priorities. There are a plethora of providers but provision is not uniform.

There are also differences between services provided for citizens and for others. The legal entitlement of migrant women to guidance and counselling, especially those not on track to become 'permitted workers', is problematic. Women more generally, who constitute the majority of the registered unemployed, are a disadvantaged group. Low economic activity rates for women in the West mean that there are large numbers of women returnees, for whom provision is variable. As significant importance is attached to qualifications in Germany, and as adult guidance in the statutory employment service is geared to past labour-market histories rather than orientations for the future, women returnees are at a particular disadvantage in negotiating their re-entry. The reconstruction of unemployed East German women as housewives rather than unemployed is a particular equity issue.

Conclusion

Vocational guidance and counselling is clearly a very important issue in Germany given:

- the upheavals in the labour market;
- the needs of migrants;
- the short shelf-life of skills acquired through the dual training system;
- the increasing drop-out rate from apprenticeships;
- the fact that, as Chisholm et al (1997, p 12) note, there is increasing dissatisfaction among both West German (one fifth) and East German employees (one third) with their current job (Statistisches Bundes-amt, 1995, p 498).

In Germany, adult guidance and placement was the legal preserve of the state employment services until very recently. Now there is some expansion in the number and range of providers, in particular third-sector organisations, largely co-funded by the EU, offering guidance alongside return-to-work preparation and courses targeted at disadvantaged groups. Guidance as an activity integrated into training and preparation for work is now available from a variety of third-sector and private-sector providers funded by these sources and the EC. Target groups for these services include the long-term unemployed, the 'hard-to-place' and returnees to the labour market.

In terms of our three models of the learning society, the dominant model in Germany is the skills growth model, with some personal development provided through third-sector projects for the disadvantaged.

Part Three
Key issues

TEN

Financing adult guidance

The case for public funding

The purpose of this chapter is to explore the various alternative methods of organising funding for guidance services, drawing on our fieldwork in the UK and other European countries. This issue is at the heart of debates about the role of guidance in a learning society. In essence it can be argued that individuals would not be able to make effective educational and vocational choices in the absence of provision of services by career guidance agencies and professionals. This case can be supported on various grounds.

First, individuals may have bounded rationality, so that without guidance, they are unable to deal with the complexities of the information that they obtain. This is a general phenomenon in market economies where information about prices and market conditions is complex.

Second, information may be costly to obtain on an individual basis, so that the transaction costs of making educational and vocational choices would discourage individuals from becoming well informed about the various opportunities available. For some types of work, simple job search strategies are appropriate. In the construction industry, for example, it is common for unskilled workers to find temporary jobs by scouting around building sites. Many jobs are found through informal networks and word of mouth. However, in more skill-intensive labour markets, more complex job search strategies are required, involving extensive research into available opportunities, and requiring the processing of large amounts of information. The same applies to searches for learning opportunities, with the addition that these searches may also need to include information on the predicted economic returns on the labour market from investment in learning activities.

Conventional public economics theory suggests that basic guidance services should be provided free of charge by the state only in the case of market failure. Information failures are widely recognised to lead to market failures, because the provision of information is not excludable. In other words, individuals would not be willing to pay for the collection and provision of information that would subsequently be available to other individuals free-of-charge. In this view, individuals left to their own devices would not be willing to pay for (the socially optimal level of) information and advice. Individuals and firms may therefore find it unprofitable to supply the necessary information on the market, in which case there will be a market failure in the provision of such information. In contrast, it is argued that in-depth guidance services are excludable, since they are specific to the individual, and there is, therefore, in principle, no market failure in this element of guidance activities. Accordingly, it is suggested that market failure occurs in the market for information about educational and career opportunities, but not in the provision of further elements of guidance services such as counselling and psychometric testing.

The 'free entry, pay to stay' model

This market-failure argument underlies the 'free entry, pay to stay' (FEPS) model, which has become the basis of government policy towards financing guidance services in the UK. The model was developed through a process of consensus building among many of the key organisations in the field (TEC National Council, 1994; Watts, 1994b; NACCEG, 1996). It suggests that basic 'entry-level' services for adults should be provided free by the state in order to support the government's aspirations to provide effective lifelong learning opportunities, and to promote efficiency in the labour market. Since for the further elements of guidance there is, allegedly, no market failure, individuals are still expected to pay fees to 'stay on' for the other elements of guidance services (see DfEE, 1998b, p 4). Free information services in this model can act as an entry port into commercial provision of in-depth guidance and counselling (for example, psychometric testing and skills assessment).

In line with this model, the Labour government has proposed that the new Information, Advice and Guidance for Adults (IAGA) Partnerships will provide free access to basic information, advice and guidance services, but that local providers should be free to decide whether or not individuals who require more in-depth counselling should pay for it:

> Ministers intend that partnerships should provide a basic information
> and advice service free of charge. Whether other services should be
> provided free should be a matter for local decision, in the light of

the overall resources available to each partnership and the priorities locally. (Circular letter issued by the DfEE, 1 April 1999)

Access to free information has been extended by the introduction of a telephone helpline service and website as part of the new Learndirect initiative. Even here, however, charges are being introduced within the website for access to diagnostic packages which start to move closer to the 'guidance' domain.

But if there is an argument in favour of free entry-level guidance, it is surely short-sighted to deny the benefits of more in-depth guidance to individuals. There are major benefits in the public provision of comprehensive adult guidance over and beyond the basic provision of information and advice.

First, users typically experience difficulty in borrowing against a prospective increase in human capital, and so would be unlikely or unable to finance relatively costly in-depth guidance services. If it is accepted that access to guidance is a public good as well as a private good (see Chapter One; also Watts, 1996b), this would justify some sort of public provision of guidance in place of 'pay-to-stay'.

Second, there is a problem associated with the quality of provision in a market for guidance services. The existence of asymmetric information about the quality of guidance services on offer (with guidance professionals having a greater insight than users into such quality) raises the possibility that the guidance market would be open to providers offering low-quality services. Users, being unable to distinguish high- and low-quality providers, would be reluctant to pay for further guidance services, and so market failure would again occur.

Third, there is the issue of equity. More socially advantaged individuals may be able to take advantage of the free information services and to self-provide the further elements of guidance, processing and analysing the information themselves, leaving less advantaged individuals to have recourse to, or suffer from lack of recourse to, the fee-charged further stages of the guidance process.

Finally, if the provision of career guidance has external effects, the social benefits of guidance may exceed the individual private benefits. External effects arise when the outcomes of guidance services spill over into other markets. This may occur whenever guidance improves the operation of the markets for learning services or for labour. We have already discussed this idea in Chapter Two, where we indicated that such external effects can be important in reducing drop-out rates from educational courses (which in many cases are publicly funded) and in reducing employee turnover rates, which will benefit employers by reducing their human resource management costs. But if fees are charged, there could be an under-supply of guidance services relative to the socially optimal level.

These considerations point to defects in the current UK approach to the development of guidance services on the FEPS model. Other alternative models will need to be explored. Our fieldwork in France, Germany, the Netherlands and Italy indicates that there are a wide variety of approaches in operation in different European countries. None of these correspond to the UK FEPS model. In the next section, we briefly indicate some of the alternative options available.

Alternatives to 'free entry, pay to stay'

In designing an institutional framework within which free and universal guidance services can be provided, there are at least two dimensions which should be considered. The first relates to the issue of who finances the services: the state, employers, individuals or some other institution. In the context of the labour market, for example, potential beneficiaries of guidance services include individuals whose job prospects are improved and whose job search costs are reduced, employers who benefit from reduced recruitment costs, and the state which benefits from reduced benefit costs if unemployment is reduced; the same mix applies in relation to the learning market. The second dimension concerns the issue of whether the services should be provided free of charge to users, or whether users should pay for guidance beyond the elementary provision of information and advice.

Our international comparative research has been designed to enable us to identify a number of alternative organisational and funding options in addition to fee paying by individuals and free provision by the state (Bartlett and Rees, 2000). The first such option is finance by employers, who stand to gain from having a well-informed and well-motivated supply of workers. The second option is through integration of finance for education, training and guidance services. The third option is through a state-funded quasi-market in which the state finances provision through competition between preferred provider organisations, which might be in the private sector or in the 'third sector', including voluntary organisations. The fourth option is through mutual or collective financing, through social self-help membership organisations such as social cooperatives, job seekers' clubs and voluntary organisations. It should be noted that these types of organisation are often supported by various EU programmes, without whose support their continued existence or even their initial setting-up would frequently be problematic. The fifth option is finance though local partnerships, which bring together a variety of local interests to finance services for the community, provided by non-profit organisations such as social cooperatives and voluntary organisations, and also by private and public-sector organisations. This partnership (or network) approach is currently being adopted by the Labour government in the UK, but in a limited form because of the government's continuing adherence to the FEPS model. We will examine each of these options in turn.

Employer-funded services

The first option is finance by employers, who stand to gain from having a well-informed and well-motivated supply of workers (since turnover rates would be reduced and productivity increased). One example of this is the employer levy system operated in France. This funds the provision of skills assessments through payments made by employers as a proportion of the wage bill. A variety of providers compete to provide guidance services to individuals, who exercise their right to a leave of absence from work for a skills assessment. The organisations which operate as providers of skills assessments in this scheme include the Inter-Institutional Skills Assessment Centres (CIBCs), the *Retravailler* organisations which provide guidance services for women returnees to the labour market, and the training agency AFPA (see Chapter Six). Through these organisations, various segments of the labour market are provided with skills assessment and associated career guidance: unemployed adults, employees, women returnees and trainees. Another example previously described, again taken from France, is APEC which provides career guidance to executives (*cadres*), and which is funded by a 0.6% levy on the wage bill.

The employer-financed guidance model could be linked to the position taken by the Trades Union Congress (TUC) in relation to financing training in the UK through a 'training levy' (TUC, 1995). Part of the funds gathered through a levy could be used to fund the provision of guidance services. There is already a levy system in operation in the construction industry in the form of the Construction Industry Training Board, and the TUC have argued for the expansion of this system into an all-inclusive levy organised as a 1-2% increase in employer

National Insurance contributions. However, there has been little discussion of the ways in which these funds could be used to support adult guidance services. The TUC seems to have endorsed the FEPS model, through which finance would be provided for a universal-access information service, but with fee-charging for more extensive guidance services. In the words of the TUC, "customised guidance could be provided on a charged basis to those who can afford to pay" (TUC, 1995, p 23). Nor is there any discussion in the TUC document of the mechanisms for assuring equality of access to guidance services, such as the right to a leave of absence for skills assessment along the lines of the French model.

A possible route for the introduction of a variant of this system in the UK might be through the introduction of a guidance component in the Individual Learning Accounts (ILAs) being introduced by the current Labour government. Under this approach, employers, the state and the individual are encouraged to fund learning on a co-investment basis. Although the Labour government's proposal focuses on the funding of learning, it could be extended to cover the funding of guidance services (see Watts, 1999a).

The problem, as we see it, with the idea of ILAs in this context is that it fails to address the essential insurance element of guidance services. Under an insurance-based approach, the emphasis would be on the risk and uncertainty that an individual faces in the labour market and in their education and employment decisions. If it is true that job insecurity is increasing and that individuals will be subjected to random disturbances to their careers throughout life, then it makes sense to think of insuring the provision of guidance services to chart a course through the transition processes between re-training and re-employment. In this view, the French system can be viewed as a form of social insurance, and avoids the problems associated with individually funded insurance systems of the type proposed through ILAs. Such individual insurance schemes, whether compulsory or voluntary (as in the case of privately purchased unemployment insurance, which after all could be extended to guidance services), imply an in-built inequality in the distribution of benefits. Those most in need of guidance would find that they have the smallest ILA funds to pay for it.

Integration of finance for education/training and guidance services

The second option is through integration of finance for education, training and guidance services. In France, the state-funded training agency, AFPA, is a provider of skills assessments, and delivers guidance alongside its training activities (see Chapter Six). In the Netherlands, good guidance services are regarded as being in the interests of the community colleges, which have financial incentives to retain students, but only if they are likely to complete their courses successfully (see Chapter Seven). In Germany, too, guidance attached to education and training provision has been growing (see Chapter Nine).

In the UK, as noted in Chapter Four, entry-level guidance in FE colleges in England has been financed through the FEFC budget. Ten per cent of this budget has been given over to entry-level guidance. However, the system has suffered from a major defect in that an FE college has not been able to claim funding for 'at entry' guidance if the individual has not enrolled on a course. The guidance provided by colleges has therefore not been independent, and there has been a temptation to encourage prospective students to enrol for the financial gain of the college, even where this might not be in the individual's interest. With the replacement of FEFC by the Learning and Skills Council, with a wider remit covering training as well as education, it seems unlikely that the funding provision for entry-level guidance will be maintained, although the provision of impartial guidance in enabling learners to choose the course or programme which is right for them seems likely to be incorporated in the inspection arrangements (OFSTED/TSC/FEFC, 2000).

State-funded quasi-markets

The third option is through a state-funded quasi-market in which the state finances provision through competition between preferred provider organisations. As indicated above, the main example of this approach is found in France, where the state employment agency, ANPE, contracts out the provision of adult guidance services on a competitive basis (see Chapter Six). In several European countries, an effective system of adult guidance is financed directly by the state. Its mission is to give everyone who registers an initial interview that provides clients with basic career guidance. Beyond this initial service, however, further guidance work is contracted out to other professional organisations.

These providers compete for contracts from ANPE to provide such services. This, therefore, represents an example of a state- funded quasi-market for adult guidance provision.

The case of the Netherlands (see Chapter Seven) presents another example of a state-funded quasi-market. Before recent market-oriented reforms, the Dutch regional guidance centres (like careers services in the UK) were centrally funded through the government budget, and delivered services free of charge to schools and to the Employment Office. Since the reforms in the early 1990s, schools have received devolved budgets, and have chosen either to contract out for the services or to supply them in-house. The guidance centres (AOBs) have lost their central funding and must compete for contracts from schools and other bodies (mainly local and regional Employment Offices). The key point is that the guidance clients concerned (trainees, unemployed, migrants) do not have to pay for the services directly, any more than they did before. Outside these groups, there are elements of an 'open' market where clients pay directly for their guidance services.

In the UK (see Chapters Four and Five), too, a quasi-market model was introduced in the provision of guidance services, mainly to young people, by requiring careers companies to enter into competition for service contracts. Another initiative developed in the UK was the funding of guidance services through the use of vouchers. These were introduced through two programmes, Gateways to Learning for unemployed people, and Skill Choice for individuals in employment. The programmes were administered largely by the TECs, and in the case of Skill Choice could be topped up by individual contributions. Evaluation studies revealed that these experiments had high transaction costs and did not give rise to the expected benefits in the form of more active choices and decision making by the beneficiaries; they were quietly dropped when the parent schemes came to a close. TECs have also contracted for adult guidance services with a range of providers but the TEC-managed quasi-market in the UK has resulted in patchy and fragmented provision.

Mutuality and cooperative societies

The fourth option is through mutual or collective financing social self-help membership organisations such as social cooperatives, job seekers' clubs and voluntary organisations. This type of approach has also been discussed by other research carried out by the Demos think-tank (Leadbeater, 1998). As we have seen, the main examples are found in

Italy, but they also exist elsewhere throughout Europe. Funding is provided by local authorities, local businesses, ESF and through the membership contributions of the clients. Typical examples are the Milanese *Orientamento Lavoro* organisation, the ORSO cooperative, and other social cooperatives working in the guidance field in Italy (see Chapter Eight). *Orientamento Lavoro* is a non-profit organisation established in 1986, within the *Retravailler* movement. Its original purpose was to provide guidance services for women labour-market returnees. Although it has now extended its scope beyond this, it is still primarily providing services to help women improve their position in the labour market.

Another example of a charitable, not-for-profit organisation providing guidance for a disadvantaged group can be found in Bremen, in Germany. *Paritäisches Bildungswerk* (see Chapter Nine) is an educational organisation largely funded by the *Land* and by ESF. It targets inter alia migrant women whose legal status (as wives of migrants) means that they are not eligible for state-provided services. Although the main focus of their activities is on general education, language development and political education, guidance and counselling is included as part of an holistic approach to personal development. The course for migrant women was set up in 1992 and is hugely oversubscribed. The pre-vocational education and training is provided with a view to the women going on to further education or training and eventually joining the labour market, by which time their legal status should have been regularised.

The origins of this approach lie in the 19th-century 'friendly societies' in the UK. These third-sector organisations have their echo in the UK in a variety of non-profit and charitable organisations, including some EGSAs (Educational Guidance Services for Adults). The first EGSA was established in Belfast in the 1970s, and others later appeared elsewhere in the UK, leading to the formation of a national association, the National Association for Educational Guidance for Adults (NAEGA). The Belfast EGSA was set up by a group of social workers to help unemployed adults find suitable training and employment opportunities. However, although they provided a useful base on which to build, EGSAs failed to command the support they needed if they were to have any significant continuing impact on the provision of adult educational guidance in the UK. Many have now disappeared or been merged into careers services or college-based services. There are also a number of other linked organisations in the UK. These voluntary organisations rely on charitable donations and a continuous search for funds from government agencies.

Local partnerships

The fifth option is finance through local partnerships, which bring together a variety of local interests to finance services for the local community, provided by non-profit voluntary-sector organisations but also by public and private-sector bodies. Examples are the *Missions Locales* in France, and organisations such as *PromoLavoro* in Italy. The aim of the *MLs* (see Chapter Six) is to work with disadvantaged youth, to help them reintegrate into society through the provision of a variety of essential welfare services, including support for housing, training and job search. As part of their function, they also provide career guidance. They are funded by a coalition of local interests, including the regional and municipal governments, as well as by the state. The *PromoLavoro* organisation (see Chapter Eight) provides guidance services to unemployed people in the town of Novara, where it was set up as a private company and financed by the Chamber of Commerce, the city council and provincial government.

In the UK, the Labour government's policy is based on the central funding of local Information, Advice and Guidance for Adults (IAGA) Partnerships. In contrast to the Conservative government's approach, the contracts are to be agreed with existing providers by negotiation, on a cooperative rather than competitive basis (DfEE, 1998b, p 7). The partnerships are to act as networks of existing provider organisations such as careers service companies, the Employment Service, TECs, local authorities, further and higher education institutions, voluntary organisations and private-sector providers with a guidance capacity. As indicated above, priority at local level is currently being given to the development of a basic information and advice service (for both employment and education issues) provided free of charge along the lines of the FEPS model, rather than to in-depth guidance services. Nonetheless, the model could be extended to cover the latter services too.

Conclusion

All these options for funding can be found in the various European countries, as well as to some extent in local initiatives in the UK that we have looked at in our research. As far as current government policy in the UK is concerned, the public provision of free entry-level information and advice services is a useful step forward. However, it is unlikely that an option based almost entirely on user fees and charges for in-depth adult guidance, as has been advocated in the UK, will be capable of supporting the widespread diffusion of lifelong guidance required to support the needs of an emerging learning society. Exactly which other options might be adopted more fully as an alternative or supplement to the UK FEPS model depends very much upon the vision of the learning society which drives policy making. It is to the definition of possible alternative visions that we will turn in our concluding chapter.

ELEVEN

Conclusion

Diversity

In Chapter One we outlined our three models of the learning society: the skills growth model, emphasising the link between skill formation and economic growth; the personal development model, which is concerned with facilitating individual self-fulfilment; and the social learning model, which emphasises the embeddedness of the learning process in the social and community context in which individuals are situated. We have argued that the skills growth model has tended to dominate the policy documents of the EC and the UK government. Among the European case studies, elements of the personal development model seem to be strongest in the French system, with its emphasis on the 'social insertion' of disadvantaged groups in society, while elements of the social learning model are strongest in Italy, despite (or perhaps because of) the marginal position of state-provided guidance services there.

The UK and Netherlands have shared a pattern of deregulation and marketisation of guidance services. Typically, providers have competed for contracts to provide services. Public money has been used to provide a public service, but one that may be provided by a private-sector supplier. As the providers need to compete successfully for such contracts, alternative sources of funding are eagerly sought.

These various approaches to provision have profound implications for adults seeking guidance in the different member states. Moreover, the respective infrastructure arrangements position providers differently in terms of their capacity to respond to EC co-funding for guidance as part of training and employment projects or other activities. The EC programmes have to be made to work with national systems of provision. Where systems of guidance are poorly developed, as in Italy, EC co-funding has been critical to the development of guidance services for adults, including the activities of newly emerging third-sector providers. Where there are strong state systems in place, such as in France and Germany, the role of the EC is more marginal. Where guidance services have been obliged to earn income from their activities through winning contracts, as in the Netherlands, providers have targeted the EC programmes to support guidance services financially; for example, the Netherlands has become one of the chief beneficiaries of the LEONARDO DA VINCI programme.

In the UK, in the context of devolution, the divergence of patterns of welfare provision that began with the marketisation of public services under the Conservative government is likely to continue. Already, the nature and level of provision of adult guidance services varies considerably across the UK. As a consequence, there are different approaches and levels of involvement with EU programmes (Bartlett and Rees, 1999). The variation in systems of contracting out in England and Scotland appears to have led to different patterns of use of EC co-funding to support adult guidance. The institutional framework in Fife (see Chapter Five) seems to be particularly favourable for accessing EC resources.

Among the growing number of third-sector providers in Germany, and in our Scottish case study, where adult guidance is provided by the local authority under a combined social and economic regeneration policy, EC funding has been used to resource the personal development model of the learning society. In many of the projects we visited, it was difficult to differentiate between the training and personal development aspects of the work. Guidance was fully integrated into a client-centred developmental approach. The third-sector providers in Germany were largely untrained in guidance but took a holistic approach to the development of the client. In the Scottish case study, on the other hand, the providers were fully trained professional guidance staff. Guidance was prioritised in this area of high unemployment and industrial restructuring as a mechanism for assisting the long-term development of the area and its people.

At the beginning of this book, we drew attention to how the marketisation of public services tends to have unforeseen effects. Two of these concern the quality of services provided, and the extent to which market principles might compromise the principle of equity.

Quality

The quality of services is inevitably linked to regulation. One of the consequences of EC co-funding becoming available for guidance services provided as part of other activities, such as training and preparation for returning to work, is that a wide range of people now provide these services. Not all of them by any means have necessarily been trained in guidance work. The quality of such services will be affected by the context within which they are provided. Breaking the link between guidance of adults and the provision of unemployment benefits in these conditions may provide – as some of our case-study respondents in Germany suggested – a more holistic and less job-oriented approach. In the Netherlands we heard how the marketisation process had created a demand for counsellors and hence for courses for training them. Colleges were keen to respond to that demand by providing short courses in guidance and counselling, but the inspection services no longer examined what was provided and the position of the professional association was consequently weakened. Barely trained people were competing for contracts, undercutting the prices of the qualified.

The French case illustrates a more systematic approach to the employment of trained and qualified guidance professionals, reflecting the more comprehensive coverage and the involvement of both the state and employers' organisations in the financing of the services. Guidance professionals were typically expected to have qualifications in psychology or related areas. A national guidance institute – *L'Institut National d'Etude du Travail et d'Orientation Professionelle* (National Institute for the Study of Work and Professional Guidance – INETOP) based in Paris – provides professional training for guidance workers. In Italy, in contrast, there are no specific training courses for guidance professionals, reflecting the underdeveloped state of the guidance services in that country.

In the UK, systematic efforts have been made to develop national occupational standards across the guidance field. A 'lead body', subsequently named CAMPAG, was set up in 1992, covering advice, advocacy, counselling, mediation and psychotherapy. In addition, organisational quality standards for use across the guidance field have been developed under the aegis of the Guidance Council, which brings together all of the several UK professional associations in the guidance field as well as 'stakeholder' bodies and observers from relevant government departments. These quality standards have now been given official status in the field of adult guidance, in the sense that by 2002 all bodies in receipt of public funding for information, advice and guidance for adults must meet the standards. In other sectors, however, the status of the standards in relation to other quality-assurance systems has not yet been resolved (Watts and Sadler, 2000).

Equity

The issue of equity affects the provision of adult guidance at a number of levels. Spatially, it is clear, particularly in the UK, that access to services for adults depends on where one lives. While some areas have invested in guidance for adults, others have not. This appears to be the case irrespective of local labour-market conditions. In France, services are tailored to the needs of different groups, and provided by different organisations. Gender is clearly a key dimension, given its importance as a signifier in the organisation of education, training and the labour market. However, there is little evidence of examples of providers seeking to combat gender stereotyping to any marked degree in their guidance activities. Rather, in Germany, unemployed women from the new *Länder* were faced with stereotypical ideas based on the norm of low economic activity rates for married women in the old *Länder*.

'Cream-skimming' has been identified as a particular feature of public services operating in quasi-markets. Certainly, among some of the third-sector providers operating in Germany and the Netherlands, the specificities of the terms of the contracts and the performance indicators put an emphasis on outcomes (in terms of numbers placed) rather than process. There may well in such cases be short-term expediencies at play in guiding individuals towards destinations that satisfy such mechanisms; these were not such a feature of the public service, where a longer-term view could be taken.

The EU is seeking to develop policies to enhance its competitiveness as a global region and to avoid the social exclusion of groups of its citizens, despite the fact that, as discussed in Chapter Three, policies designed to achieve the former may be at odds with those designed to achieve the latter. There is a growing concern at EC level about the position of women in the labour market, fuelled by both of these strategic goals. On the one hand, women constitute the majority of the unskilled and low skilled, as well as the majority of the unemployed and economically inactive from whom, in the context of a declining birth rate, new entrants to the labour market are expected to come. On the other hand, given the decline of the welfare state in many of the EU member states including the UK, it is increasingly clear that women will need to be members of the workforce in order to ensure their contributions to occupational pensions. Women and their children are identified as comprising the bulk of the socially excluded (EC, 1994b). The concern with gender equality in education, training and work as expressed in the economic, social and teaching and learning White Papers

(EC, 1994a, 1994b, 1996a) is thus driven by the business case as well as well as by concerns for social justice.

However, these White Papers, as we saw in Chapter Three, were not based on an analysis of the gendering of the labour market. Rather, women were identified as a group with 'special needs' to be addressed through medium-term action programmes. Indeed, a review of the participation of women in activities co-financed by the ESF makes the point that 'supplementary measures' such as childcare should be seen as integral to economic development and not simply as add-on policies addressing women's needs. More recently, however, the EC has committed itself to a three-pronged approach to fostering gender equality (Rees, 1998b):

- equal treatment of men and women – to be achieved through Directives;
- positive action measures – to address the disadvantages experienced by women;
- gender mainstreaming – where gender equality is integrated into all EC programmes, policies and actions.

The mainstreaming policy was mooted in a Communication (EC, 1996b) and has since assumed a more strategic importance, especially in the Structural Funds. It is, however, complemented by the other two approaches. For example, most recently there have been directives on parental leave. A new Fifth Medium Term Action Programme on Equal Treatment of Men and Women allows for co-funding of positive action and mainstreaming measures. These approaches were formalised in the Amsterdam Treaty where gender mainstreaming was identified as the key new policy approach to gender equality. At the same time, a commitment was made to equal treatment on the grounds of race and ethnic origin, religious belief, sexual orientation, disability, and age.

In our examination of guidance services in the UK, France, the Netherlands, Italy and Germany, it was, for the most part, an equal-treatment approach that dominated who received services. That is to say, men and women were equally entitled to receive services. However, there were exceptions to this, as in the case of women migrants in Germany married to migrants. In all the member states we studied, there were examples of positive-action projects designed to address the special needs of women. One of the main shortcomings of the equal-treatment approach is that it tends to be interpreted as treating women as the same as, rather than as equal to, men. Hence, in Germany, for example, while women share an equal entitlement to men to make use of adult guidance services, the state system does not accommodate very successfully the needs of women where these are different to those of men. This is shown most clearly in the case of women returnees. Here it tends to be positive-action measures that are used to address their needs. By their very nature, such measures tend to be piecemeal, temporary and not available on a universal basis. It is third-sector providers, such as the *Retravailler* group of organisations in France, Italy and some other EU countries, that have sought to fill this gap. As we saw among our case study providers, the demand for such services where they exist is substantial. What we did not find among our case-study countries was much evidence of a mainstreaming approach to gender equality.

The two examples of countries where adult guidance services have moved most strongly towards marketisation – the UK and the Netherlands – have shown that the mechanisms of financing adult guidance together with performance-related target setting can inhibit longer-term guidance work with adults that addresses the equality dimension. In Germany, the state-run employment service operates an equal treatment approach and the third sector provides specialist positive-action projects. In France, the approach is one of a series of providers targeting the needs of different groups according to their status in the labour market. While *Retravailler* was originally concerned only with women, it has extended its remit to accommodate men. In Italy, we saw minimal state provision and a plethora of community-based providers open to men and women.

It is too early to determine to what extent the gender mainstreaming policy of the EU is affecting the delivery of policies on the ground through, for example, projects co-resourced by the Structural Funds. However, reports on progress since the mainstreaming communication, and the annual reports on equal opportunities in the member states, point to problems of lack of awareness, lack of expertise, lack of dedicated budgets and a lack of clarity as to what mainstreaming means. It also remains to be seen to what extent the commitment of the current Labour government to equality will percolate through to the checks and levers that frame the provision of adult guidance services in the UK. So far, mainstreaming has been adopted as official government policy and a women's unit has been set up in the Cabinet Office. There have been policies on combating institutionalised racism in the public sector (emanating from the MacPherson Inquiry on the death of Stephen Lawrence). The Disability Rights Commission has been set up. The publication of a code of practice for employers on good practice in addressing sexual orientation at work is imminent. As yet, however, there is little sign of these moves filtering through to the delivery of guidance services for adults.

In our view, it is mainstreaming practice that is most likely to deliver adult guidance services that address the needs of all groups and combat stereotyping in the education, training and labour markets. This needs to be complemented by the legal right of access to equal treatment, together with positive-action measures to develop a client-centred test-bed of good practice. Mainstreaming so far has focused on gender equality and clearly needs to be extended to accommodate all the equality dimensions.

Conclusion

We return finally to the three distinct models of the learning society outlined in Chapter One. The first was the 'skills growth model', which emphasises the link between skill formation and economic growth. The improvement of the skills of the labour force is widely seen as a critical determinant of the international competitiveness of the economy. Barro (1997) supports this hypothesis. In a comparative study of growth among 114 countries over 30 years from 1960 to 1990, Barro showed a positive relation between the extent of secondary and higher education and economic growth. Rapid technological change requires continual re-training and re-skilling of the labour force to maintain an economy's position in the international pecking order. In this view, career guidance is instrumental and deterministic, providing a brokerage service for individuals in search of particular jobs or training courses.

This view seems to have dominated official thinking in the UK and the Netherlands, and at the supranational level, in the EU as well. Not surprisingly, given the economistic and market-oriented basis of the skills growth model of the learning society, marketisation and deregulation have been the hallmarks of this approach to the reform of guidance service delivery in these two countries. The position of the EU is rather more complex, since although it has accepted the skills growth model in relation to its competitiveness goals, it also accepts the personal development model, and indeed also to some extent the social learning approach, in relation to its goals of promoting gender equality and social cohesion. Its actions and programmes, while based on a competitive contracting mechanism, have in practice tended to favour and support experimental and innovative guidance programmes carried out by a wide variety of third-sector providers.

The second model was the 'personal development model', which is more concerned with facilitating individual self-fulfilment by provision of resources to enable individuals to make informed choices about their preferred modes of participation in learning and work. This model links more closely to the new view of career outlined in Chapter One, and implies a more client-centred and voluntaristic role for the guidance services. It highlights a concern for equity, and the importance of individual self-fulfilment through the learning experience. This approach is characteristic of the French concern with the 'social insertion' of disadvantaged groups, and is evident in the involvement of the 'social partners' (employers, trades unions and the state) in many of the local initiatives, such as the *MLs*, and in the funding of the skills assessment programme. The newly emerging and innovative approaches in Germany, which closely involve third-sector providers, also fall into this pattern, although the German government's policy is clearly more sympathetic to the skills growth model.

The third model, which we called the 'social learning model', emphasises the embeddedness of the learning process in the social and community context in which individuals are situated. This view emphasises the role of social connectivity, and the institutions of trust and cooperation, in providing the foundations on which market-based economies can flourish and prosper. The role of collaborative learning and 'social capital', which draws on community resources and institutions in promoting lifelong learning, has been stressed by Schuller and Field (1998). The model implies a more action-oriented role for guidance services, in which guidance providers work alongside individuals rather than acting as independent experts. Examples can be found in the Italian experience with social cooperatives in which disadvantaged individuals work alongside guidance workers in a cooperative enterprise.

Coffield (1998, p 9) has suggested that:

> ... these three models are a convenient device for making sense not only of much of the research conducted by the fourteen projects which make up The Learning Society Programme, but also of the new Labour government's vision for lifelong learning, as detailed in The Learning Age. (DfEE, 1998a)

Clearly, these different conceptions of a learning society imply radically different approaches to policy (see Rees and Bartlett, 1999a). However, in all three cases, there is a growing consensus on the importance of career guidance for adults as an active and central element in its development.

In the UK (as also in the EU), policy towards lifelong learning and lifelong guidance has so far been informed mainly by the skills growth model. However, in our view, a wider conception of the learning society is needed, encompassing elements of the personal development and social learning approaches. In relation to the funding options outlined in Chapter Ten, the former could be promoted using our first financing option by an extension of the individual learning accounts proposals to incorporate a guidance element, to include employer contributions as proposed by the TUC, and to draw on the French experience with skills assessments. The latter could be supported by our fourth financing option, developing mutual and collective forms of organisation and funding, and could draw on experiences developed elsewhere, for example in the Italian social cooperatives. In order to succeed, however, the framework surrounding the provision of guidance services for adults needs to build in commitment to ensuring the highest standards of quality and equity.

References

ACACE (Advisory Council for Adult and Continuing Education) (1979) *Links to learning*, Leicester: ACACE.

Argyris, C. (1960) *Understanding organizational behaviour*, Homewood, IL: Dorsey.

Ball, C. (ed) (1993) *Guidance matters: Developing a national strategy for guidance in learning and work*, London: Royal Society of Arts.

Banks, J.A.G., Raban, A.J. and Watts, A.G. (1990) 'The single European market and its implications for educational and vocational guidance services', *International Journal for the Advancement of Counselling*, vol 13, pp 275-94.

Barro, R.J. (1997) *Determinants of economic growth: A cross-country empirical study*, Cambridge, MA: MIT Press.

Bartlett, W. (1993) 'The evolution of workers' cooperatives in southern Europe: a comparative perspective', in C. Karlsson, B. Johanisson and D. Storey (eds) *Small business dynamics: International, national and regional perspectives*, London: Routledge, pp 57-76.

Bartlett, W. and Rees, T. (1998) *Adult guidance and the learning society*, Final Report to ESRC, Project No L12351007, Swindon: Economic and Social Research Council.

Bartlett, W. and Rees, T. (1999) 'Adult guidance services for a learning society? Evidence from England', in F. Coffield (ed) *Speaking truth to power: Research and policy on lifelong learning*, Bristol: The Policy Press, pp 73-85.

Bartlett, W. and Rees, T. (2000) 'The variable contribution of guidance services in different types of learning societies', in F. Coffield (ed) *Differing visions of a Learning Society: Research findings, Volume 1*, Bristol: The Policy Press, pp 139-66.

Baumol, W., Panzar, J. and Willig, R. (1982) *Contestable markets and the theory of industry structure*, San Diego, CA: Harcourt, Brace, Jovanovich.

Beck, U. (1992) *The risk society*, London: Sage Publications.

BfA (Bundesanstalt für Arbeit) (1991) *Vocational guidance in the Federal Republic of Germany*, Nuremberg: BfA.

BfA (1996) *Berufsberatung 1994/5*, Nuremberg: BfA.

Borzaga, C. (ed) (2000) *Capitale umano e qualita del lavoro nei servizi sociali*, Roma: Fondazione Italiana per il Volontariato.

Borzaga, C. and Chiesa, A. (1997) 'Counselling services in Italy', Paper presented to the *International ESRC Project Workshop on Guidance Services and the Learning Society*, University of Bristol, 11-12 September.

Brewer, J.M. (1942) *History of vocational guidance*, New York, NY: Harper.

Bridges, W. (1995) *Jobshift: How to prosper in a workplace without jobs*, London: Nicholas Brealey.

Burgess, S. and Rees, H. (1996) 'Job tenure in Britain 1975-1992', *Economic Journal*, vol 1, no 6, pp 334-44.

Burgess, S. and Rees, H. (1997) *A disaggregate analysis of the evolution of job tenure in Britain 1975-93*, Centre for Economic Policy Research Discussion Paper 1711, London: CEPR.

CBI (Confederation of British Industry) (1989) *Towards a skills revolution*, London: CBI.

CEC (Commission of the European Communities) (1996) *Employment in Europe 1996*, Luxembourg: Office for Official Publications of the European Communities.

Chatrik, B. (1997) 'Who's running the Careers Service now?', *Working Brief*, February, pp 17-20.

Chisholm, L., Friesse, M., Thiessen, B. and Struckmeyer, S. (1997) 'Guidance services and the learning society: adult guidance and counselling services in Germany', Paper presented to the *International ESRC Guidance Services and the Learning Society Project Seminar*, University of Bristol, 11-12 September.

Clayton, P., Creté, N., Flejabeitia, C., Friese, M. and Ward, H. (1997) 'Vocational guidance and counselling and women returners in Germany', in L. Chisholm (ed) *Getting in, climbing up and breaking through: Women returners and vocational guidance and counselling*, Bristol: The Policy Press, pp 44-64.

Coffield, F. (1998) 'Introduction: lifelong learning as social control', in F. Coffield (ed) *Why's the beer always stronger up North? Studies of lifelong learning in Europe*, Bristol: The Policy Press, pp 1-12.

Coffield, F. (ed) (2000) *Differing visions of a Learning Society: Research findings, Volumes 1 and 2*, Bristol: The Policy Press.

Collin, A. and Watts, A.G. (1996) 'The death and transfiguration of career – and of career guidance?', *British Journal of Guidance and Counselling*, vol 24, no 3, pp 385-98.

Commission on Public Policy and British Business (1997) *Promoting prosperity: A business agenda for Britain*, London: Vintage.

Connelly, G., Milburn, T., Thomson, S. and Edwards, R. (1998) 'Guiding adults impartially: a Scottish study', *Studies in the Education of Adults*, vol 30, no 2, pp 142-55.

Coopers & Lybrand (1994) *Gateways to learning national evaluation: Final report*, London: Coopers & Lybrand.

CSJ (Commission on Social Justice)/IPPR (Institute of Public Policy Research) (1994) *Social justice: Strategies for national renewal*, London: IPPR/Vintage.

Danvers, F. and Monsanson, N. (1997) 'Guidance services and the learning society: adult guidance and counselling services in France', Paper presented to the *International ESRC Project Workshop on Guidance Services and the Learning Society*, University of Bristol, 11-12 September.

Daws, P.P. (1972) 'The role of the careers teacher', in J. Hayes and B. Hopson (eds) *Careers guidance: The role of the school in vocational development*, London: Heinemann, pp 1-9.

Dell'Aringa, C. and Lodovici, M.S. (1997) 'Policies for the unemployment and social shock absorbers: the Italian experience', in B. Palier (ed) *Comparing social welfare systems in Southern Europe*, vol 3, Paris: MIRE, pp 443-66.

DES (Department of Education and Science) (1973) *Careers education in secondary schools*, Education Survey 18, London: HMSO.

DfEE (Department for Education and Employment) (1998a) *The Learning Age: A renaissance for a new Britain*, London: DfEE.

DfEE (1998b) *Local information, advice and guidance for adults in England – Towards a national framework*, Sheffield: DfEE.

Doogan, K. (1998) 'The impact of European integration on labour market institutions', *International Planning Studies*, vol 3, no 1, pp 57-74.

Ducatel, K., Shapiro, H., Rees, T. and Weinkopf, C. (2000) 'Towards the learning labor market', in K. Ducatel, J. Webster and W. Herrmann (eds) *The information society in Europe: Work and life in an age of globalization*, Maryland: Rowman and Littlefield, pp 141-71.

Earle, J. (1986) *The Italian cooperative movement*, London: Allen and Unwin.

EC (European Commission) (1994a) *Growth, competitiveness, employment: The challenges and ways forward into the 21st century*, White Paper, Luxembourg: Office for Official Publications of the European Communities.

EC (1994b) *European social policy: A way forward for the Union*, White Paper, Luxembourg: Office for Official Publications of the European Communities.

EC (1994c) *European handbook for guidance counsellors*, Luxembourg: Office for Official Publications of the European Communities.

EC (1995) *The European dimension in vocational guidance*, Luxembourg: Office for Official Publications of the European Communities.

EC (1996a) *Teaching and learning: Towards the learning society*, Luxembourg: Office for Official Publications of the European Communities.

EC (1996b) *Incorporating equal opportunities for women and men into all Community policies and activities*, Communication from the Commission, 21 December, COM(96) final (the 'mainstreaming' communication), Brussels: EC.

EC (1998) 'Job turnover in the European Union', in EC *Employment in Europe 1997: Analysis of key issues*, Luxembourg: Office for Official Publications of the European Communities.

EC (1999a) *The European Employment Strategy and the ESF in 1998*, Luxembourg: Office for Official Publications of the European Communities.

EC (1999b) *Modernising the European public employment services – three key documents*, Luxembourg: Office for Official Publications of the European Communities.

EC (1999c) *Employment performance in the member states: Employment rates report 1998*, Luxembourg: Office for Official Publications of the European Communities.

ECCTIS 2000 (Educational Counselling and Credit Transfer Information Service) (1998) *Lifelong learning: A survey of second-year undergraduates 1997/98*, Cheltenham: ECCTIS 2000.

Ertelt, B.J. (1992) *Tätigkeitsprofile beruflicher berater in der Bundesrepublik Deutschland*, Berlin: CEDEFOP.

Ertelt, B.J., Heller, K.A. and Plant, P. (1993) *Educational and vocational guidance services in the Federal Republic of Germany*, Report to the Commission of the European Communities Task Force Human Resources Education, Training and Youth (now the EC Education, Training and Youth Directorate).

Field, J. (1997) 'The European Union and the learning society: contested sovereignty in an age of globalisation', in F. Coffield (ed) *A national strategy for lifelong learning*, Newcastle upon Tyne: Department of Education, University of Newcastle, pp 95-111.

Fryer, R.H. (1997) *Learning for the twenty-first century*, First Report of the National Advisory Group for Continuing Education and Lifelong Learning, London: NAGCELL.

Fukuyama, F. (1995) *Trust: The social virtues and the creation of new prosperity*, New York, NY: Free Press.

Gregg, P. and Wadsworth, J. (1995) 'A short history of labour turnover, job tenure and job security, 1975-93', *Oxford Review of Economic Policy*, vol 11, no 1, pp 73-90.

Hakim, C. (1994) *We are all self-employed*, San Francisco, CA: Berrett-Koehler.

Hawthorn, R. (1996a) 'Other sources of guidance on learning and work', in A.G. Watts, J. Killeen, J.M. Kidd and R. Hawthorn, *Rethinking careers education and guidance: Theory, policy and practice*, London: Routledge, pp 173-85.

Hawthorn, R. (1996b) 'Careers work in further and adult education', in A.G. Watts, B. Law, J. Killeen, J.M. Kidd and R. Hawthorn, *Rethinking careers education and guidance: Theory, policy and practice*, London: Routledge, pp 112-26.

Heginbotham, H. (1951) *The Youth Employment Service*, London: Methuen.

Hermanns, K. (1992) BIZ 91-Ergebnisse der Repräsentativen Befragung von Benutzern der BIZ – Mediotheken in den alten Bundesländern, *ibv* 12/1992, pp 841-6.

Herriot, P. and Pemberton, C. (1995) *New deals: The revolution in managerial careers*, Chichester: Wiley.

HMI (Her Majesty's Inspectorate) (1992) *Survey of guidance 13-19 in schools and sixth form colleges*, London: Department of Education and Science.

Hutton, W. (1995) *The state we're in*, London: Jonathan Cape.

ICG (Institute of Careers Guidance) (1996) *Careers guidance for adults: A survey by the Institute of Careers Guidance of guidance work with adults by careers services in the United Kingdom*, Stourbridge: ICG.

IFAPLAN (1987) *Guidance and the school*, Brussels: IFAPLAN.

Inkson, K. (1995) 'Effects of changing economic conditions on managerial job changes and career patterns', *British Journal of Management*, vol 6, pp 183-94.

Irving, B. and Barker, V. (1999) *A New Deal? Meeting the career guidance needs of the long-term unemployed*, Swanley: College of Guidance Studies.

Jackson, H. and Haughton, L. (1998) *Adult guidance in community settings*, NICEC Briefing, Cambridge: Careers Research and Advisory Centre.

Kanter, R.M. (1989) *When giants learn to dance*, New York, NY: Simon and Schuster.

Keep, E. and Mayhew, K. (1996) 'Towards a learning society – definition and measurement', *Policy Studies*, vol 17, no 3, pp 225-32.

Keller, F.J. and Viteles, M. S. (1937) *Vocational guidance throughout the world*, London: Cape.

Kessler, I. and Undy, R. (1996) *The new employment relationship: Examining the psychological contract*, London: Institute of Personnel and Development.

Kidd, J.M. (1996) 'Career planning within work organisations', in A.G. Watts, B. Law, J. Killeen, J.M. Kidd and R. Hawthorn, *Rethinking careers education and guidance: Theory, policy and practice*, London: Routledge, pp 142-54.

Killeen, J. and Kidd, J.M. (1996) 'The Careers Service', in A.G. Watts, B. Law, J. Killeen, J.M. Kidd and R. Hawthorn, *Rethinking careers education and guidance: Theory, policy and practice*, London: Routledge, pp 155-72.

Killeen, J., White, M. and Watts, A.G. (1992) *The economic value of careers guidance*, London: Policy Studies Institute.

Law, B. (1996a) 'Developing careers programmes in organisations', in A.G. Watts, B. Law, J. Killeen, J.M. Kidd and R. Hawthorn, *Rethinking careers education and guidance: Theory, policy and practice*, London: Routledge, pp 307-30.

Law, B. (1996b) 'Recording achievement and action planning', in A.G. Watts, B. Law, J. Killeen, J.M. Kidd and R. Hawthorn, *Rethinking careers education and guidance: Theory, policy and practice*, London: Routledge, pp 247-68.

Leadbeater, C. (1998) *The employee mutual*, London: Demos.

Le Grand, J. and Bartlett, W. (eds) (1993) *Quasi-markets and social policy*, London: Macmillan.

Levitas, R. (1996) 'The concept of social exclusion and the new Durkheimian hegemony', *Critical Social Policy*, vol 16, no 1, pp 5-20.

Marks, H. (1975) 'Careers guidance in further education', *Careers Bulletin*, Spring, pp 36-40.

McNair, S. (1990) 'Guidance and the education and training market', in A.G. Watts (ed) *Guidance and educational change*, Cambridge: Careers Research and Advisory Centre/Hobsons, pp 14-18.

Meijers, F. (1995) *Arbeidsidentiteit: Studie- en beroepskeuze in de post-industriele samenleving* (Career identity: careers guidance in the post-industrial society), Alphen aan den Rijn: Samsom H.D. Tjeenk Willink.

Meijers, F. (1997) 'Adult guidance services in the Netherlands', Paper presented to the *International ESRC Guidance Services and the Learning Society Project Seminar*, held at University of Bristol, 11-12 September.

Mizrahi-Tchernonog, V. (1991) *Gestion des politiques sociales locales: analyse du recours communal aux associations*, Paris: Pantheon Sorbonne, Laboratoire d'Economie Sociale.

NACCEG (National Advisory Council for Careers and Educational Guidance) (1996) *Consultation paper on a national strategy for adult guidance*, London: Royal Society of Arts.

NCGE (National Centre for Guidance in Education) (1997) *Guidance in the information society*, Dublin: NCGE.

Oakeshott, M. (1990) *Educational guidance and curriculum change*, London: Further Education Unit/Unit for the Development of Adult Continuing Education.

OFSTED/TSC/FEFC (Office for Standards in Education/Training Standards Council/Further Education Funding Council) (2000) *Inspecting post-16 education and training: Informal consultation on the common inspection framework*, London: DfEE.

OECD (Organisation for Economic Co-operation and Development) (1996) *OECD jobs strategy: Enhancing the effectiveness of active labour market policies*, Paris: OECD.

Périer, J. (1990) *Retravailler: Une méthode à vivre*, Paris: Editions Entente.

Porter, M. (1990) *The competitive advantage of nations*, London: Macmillan.

Putnam, R.D. (1993a) 'The prosperous community: social capital and economic growth', *The American Prospect*, Spring, pp 35-42.

Putnam, R.D. (1993b) *Making democracy work: Civic traditions in modern Italy*, Princeton, NJ: Princeton University Press.

Rainbird, H. (1993) 'Vocational education and training', in M. Gold (ed) *The social dimension: Employment policy in the European Community*, London: Macmillan, pp 184-202.

Rawls, J. (1972) *A theory of justice*, Oxford: Oxford University Press.

Rees, T, (1998a) 'Social exclusion and equal opportunities', *International Planning Studies*, vol 3, no 1, pp 15-34.

Rees, T. (1998b) *Mainstreaming equality in the European Union*, London: Routledge.

Rees, T. and Bartlett, W. (1999a) 'Models of guidance services in the learning society: the case of the Netherlands', in F. Coffield (ed) *Why's the beer always stronger up North?: Studies of lifelong learning in Europe*, Bristol: The Policy Press, pp 21-30.

Rees, T. and Bartlett, W. (1999b) 'Adult guidance services in the European learning society: a Scottish case study', *Studies in the Education of Adults*, vol 31, no 1, pp 21-34.

Rees, T., Bartlett, W. and Watts, A.G. (1999) 'The marketisation of guidance services in Germany, France and Britain', *Journal of Education and Work*, vol 12, no 1, pp 5-20.

Reich, R. (1992) *The work of nations*, New York, NY: Vintage.

Roberts, K. (1977) 'The social conditions, consequences and limitations of careers guidance', *British Journal of Guidance and Counselling*, vol 5, no 1, pp 1-9.

Rodger, A. (1952) *The seven point plan*, London: National Institute of Industrial Psychology.

Rogers, C. (1965) *Client-centered therapy*, Boston, MA: Houghton Mifflin.

Rolfe, H. (1999) *Gender equality and the careers service*, Manchester: Equal Opportunities Commission.

Rubery, J., Smith, M. and Fagan, C. (1999) *Women's employment in Europe: Trends and prospects*, London: Routledge.

Schuller, T. and Field, J. (1998) 'Social capital, human capital and the learning society', *International Journal of Lifelong Education*, vol 17, no 4, pp 226-35.

Scottish Executive (1999) *Opportunities and choice: Consultation paper*, Edinburgh: Scottish Executive.

Scottish Office (1998) *Opportunity Scotland: A paper on lifelong learning*, Edinburgh: Scottish Office.

SCAGES (Standing Conference of Associations for Guidance in Educational Settings) (1993) 'Statement of principles and definitions', in C. Ball (ed) *Guidance matters: Developing a national strategy for guidance in learning and work*, London: Royal Society of Arts, pp 36-8.

Statistishes Bundesamt (Hrsg) (1995) *Datenreport 1994*, Bonn: Schriftenreihe der Bundeszentrale für Politische Bilding, Band 325, Aktualisierter Nachdruck.

Stoney, S.M. and Scott, V.M. (1984) *Careers guidance in colleges and polytechnics*, Windsor: NFER-Nelson.

Storey, D. (1994) *Understanding the small business sector*, London: Routledge.

Super, D.E. (1957) *The psychology of careers*, New York, NY: Harper and Row.

TEC National Council (1994) *Individual commitment to lifetime learning*, London: TEC National Council.

TUC (Trades Union Congress) (1995) *Funding lifelong learning: A strategy to deliver the National Education and Training Targets*, London: TUC.

UDACE (Unit for the Development of Adult Continuing Education) (1986) *The challenge of change*, Leicester: National Institute of Adult Continuing Education.

University Grants Committee (1964) *University appointments boards* (The Heyworth Report), London: HMSO.

Walsh, K. (1995) *Public services and market mechanisms: Competition, contracting and the new public management*, London: Macmillan.

Waterman, R.H. Jr, Waterman, J.A. and Collard, B.A. (1994) 'Towards a career-resilient workforce', *Harvard Business Review*, vol 72, July–August, pp 87–95.

Watts, A.G. (1977) 'Careers education in higher education: principles and practice', *British Journal of Guidance and Counselling*, vol 5, no 2, pp 167–84.

Watts, A.G. (1980) 'Educational and careers guidance services for adults: II. A review of current provision', *British Journal of Guidance and Counselling*, vol 8, no 2, pp 188–202.

Watts, A.G. (1992) 'Careers guidance services in a changing Europe', *International Journal for the Advancement of Counselling*, vol 15, no 4, pp 201–7.

Watts, A.G. (1994a) *Lifelong career development: Towards a national strategy for careers education and guidance*, CRAC Occasional Paper, Cambridge: Careers Research and Advisory Centre.

Watts, A.G. (1994b) *A strategy for developing careers guidance services for adults*, CRAC Occasional Paper, Cambridge: Careers Research and Advisory Centre.

Watts, A.G. (1995) 'Applying market principles to the delivery of careers guidance services: a critical review', *British Journal of Guidance and Counselling*, vol 23, no 1, pp 69–81.

Watts, A.G. (1996a) *Careerquake*, London: Demos.

Watts, A.G. (1996b) 'Careers guidance and public policy', in A.G. Watts, B. Law, J. Killeen, J.M. Kidd and R. Hawthorn, *Rethinking careers education and guidance: Theory, policy and practice*, London: Routledge, pp 380–91.

Watts, A.G. (1997) *Strategic directions for careers services in higher education*, NICEC Project Report, Cambridge: Careers Research and Advisory Centre.

Watts, A.G. (1999a) *Reshaping career development for the 21st century*, CeGS Occasional Paper, Derby: Centre for Guidance Studies, University of Derby.

Watts, A.G. (1999b) *Home internationals: Adult guidance policy developments in Britain and Ireland*, CRAC/NICEC Conference Briefing, Cambridge: Careers Research and Advisory Centre.

Watts, A.G. and Kidd, J.M. (2000) 'Guidance in the United Kingdom: Past, present and future', *British Journal of Guidance and Counselling*, vol 28, no 4, pp 485-502.

Watts, A.G. and Sadler, J. (2000) *Quality guidance: A sectoral analysis*, NICEC project report, Cambridge: Careers Research and Advisory Centre.

Watts, A.G. and Van Esbroeck, R. (1998) *New skills for new futures: Higher education guidance and counselling services in the European Union*, Brussels: VUB University Press.

Watts, A.G. and Young, M. (1997) 'Models of student guidance in a changing 14-19 education and training system', in A. Hodgson and K. Spours (eds) *Dearing and beyond: 14-19 qualifications, frameworks and systems*, London: Kogan Page, pp 1, 8-60.

Watts, A.G., Dartois, C. and Plant, P. (1988) *Educational and vocational guidance services for the 14-25 age group in the European Community*, Maastricht: Presses Interuniversitaires Européennes.

Watts, A.G., Guichard, J., Plant, P. and Rodriguez, M.L. (1993) *Educational and vocational guidance in the European Community*, Luxembourg: Office for Official Publications of the European Communities.

Wilkinson, R.G. (1996) *Unhealthy societies: The afflictions of inequality*, London: Routledge.

Wilson, P.A. (1997) 'Building social capital: a learning agenda for the twenty-first century', *Urban Studies*, vol 34, nos 5-6, pp 745-60.

Appendix: Methodological note

English and Scottish case studies

The case studies were based on interviews with key actors, visits to providers where we interviewed managers, and the analysis of documents and statistics, including some provided by respondents about their organisations.

Regular contact was maintained with key actors in the Department for Education and Employment (DfEE) and the Institute of Careers Guidance (ICG). Interviews were also conducted with guidance professionals and other civil servants in the DfEE and Scottish Office.

Providers we interviewed included managers in the new careers companies, TECs and LECs, local authorities, further and higher education, the probation service, providers in the voluntary and private sectors, the armed forces, and the Employment Service. Altogether, 56 in-depth interviews were carried out in the five case-study areas. The interviews were conducted by Bartlett and Rees who prepared transcripts.

France, the Netherlands, Italy and Germany

The fieldwork for the case-study countries was organised in conjunction with a consultant in each country, whose names are listed in the acknowledgements. The consultants prepared background papers for the research team on adult guidance services in their respective countries, arranged the interviews with key actors, and accompanied the relevant main author (Bartless or Rees) on the fieldwork visits and discussed the findings with them. In each member state, interviews were conducted with about 12 respondents, mainly from the appropriate government departments, the public employment service, public, private and third-sector providers, and representatives from professional associations of guidance counsellors. Background information was provided and analysed together with statistical data.

Validation

During the course of the project, regular presentations were made to the ICG annual conferences and training workshops on adult guidance, where participants provided helpful feedback on our emerging lines of approach in analysing the data. In addition, we convened a seminar of international experts in the University of Bristol where, together with our national experts, we debated the results and their implications.

For further information on the methodology, see Bartlett and Rees (1998).